CUB0867988

"Mama, you have a Bald Head!"

Thriving in the Face
of Breast Cancer

LISA M. PHILLIPS, M.S. CCC/SLP

This memoir is available at special quantity discounts for bulk purchases for sales promotions, premiums, fund-raising or educational use. Book excerpts can also be created to fit special needs.

For details, email: Lisa Phillips, M.S. CCC/SLP at lisamphillips@gmail.com.

Copyright © 2010 by Lisa Phillips, M.S. CCC/SLP

Reviewed by Shauna Cotte, M. Ed.

Cover Design by Leslie Bunnell
http://www.bunnelldesign.com/

Cover Photograph © 2010 Alexa Pappas
alexapappas@charter.net.

All rights reserved. No part of this publication may be reproduced or transmitted in any form or by any means, electronic or mechanical, including photocopying, recording, or any other storage and retrieval system, without written permission from the author.

PRINTING HISTORY

Paperback Edition / October 2010
Charleston, South Carolina

Paperback ISBN: 1-453-67287-7

Library of Congress Cataloging-in-Publication Data

Phillips, Lisa.
    Mama, you have a Bald Head : thriving in the face of breast
    cancer/ Lisa Phillips, M.S. CCC/SLP
    ISBN 1-453-67287-7
    1. Phillips, Lisa. 2. Breast Cancer patients – United States –
    memoir. I. Title

PRINTED IN THE UNITED STATES OF AMERICA

"I Need You Forever"

- Bryce Phillips

"I need you forever..." the words of my adoring, intelligent and loving little boy, Bryce. Today we were having dinner, and he lightheartedly threw his arms around my neck and exclaimed, "I love you mom. I need you forever." Moments like these are the ones that I cherish and cherish and cherish. Bryce could have asked for just about anything after that display of emotion, and it would have been his. Though already in the last few days, he has magically acquired four new water color-changing cars. A puppet master on a mission – that's my son. Overall, another healthy and strong day seasoned with a sprinkle of shut-eye throughout.

"Mama, you have a Bald Head!"

Thriving in the Face
of Breast Cancer

This memoir is dedicated to:

My husband, Dennis,
who stood by me during every step of this journey, and who always said the right words at the right time and supported my every decision. With each passing day, we learn more from each other and grow even closer. In this memoir he states that I am his hero, but he is mine. He is also the unsung hero of this journey, and I will always love him from the very bottom of my heart for all that he is and all that we have and will become together.

Dennis: Thank you for being you. Thank you for keeping me strong when I wasn't so sure, and thank you for being the most loving and positive husband and father. K&H. Love Your Girl, Lili xoxo

My son, Bryce,
who is the light of my life – a beacon of
optimism, smiles and laughs. He is the
inspiration behind the title of this
memoir, as his many expressions kept
me in positive spirits throughout the
days. Along the way he would tell me,
"I need you forever; you can do this,"
"You are stuck with me" and "Is my
hug too tight?" At the tender age of
two and three, he gave me more
strength than he could ever realize.

Bryce: I will always love you.
Remember that when life throws you
lemons, make lemonade. Work hard,
never settle and never give up.
Persevere and learn from your
experiences – positive or otherwise.
Thank you for loving me
unconditionally. You are my best
friend and always will be – even when
you are old, married and with your
own kids. Forever, Mom xoxo

**And the Guardian Angel, who saved
my life.**
I will always be thankful for you,
wherever you are.

Acknowledgements

I am eternally thankful for my mom and dad, Donna and Edward. Words cannot describe my good fortune in having parents who are wonderful teachers, supporters and motivators. Being a parent myself, I cannot envision handling a situation like this one with as much grace as my mom and dad. Even when I knew it was difficult for them, they were always there for me when I needed them most. I am truly lucky. I love you mom and dad, so much!

To my brother, Eddy, and his wife, Jennifer, thank you for keeping me busy with your wedding planning and maintaining positivity in a time that could have been otherwise been quite bleak. I love you both!

I must also acknowledge my mother-in-law, Debby and father-in-law, Dennis Sr. for helping at a moment's notice, taking notes to make sure I had all the details straight and coming over with meals, laughs and encouragement to "just keeping swimming."

Many thanks to Danielle, my sister-in-law, for her love and surprise care packages from sunny Miami.

Further thanks are given to my Aunt Helen and Aunt Donna. This dynamic duo was not only there when I needed a babysitter or a good laugh but also during music classes, nap times, morning times and night times – you name it!

To Nancy C., my very best friend – Simply put, I love you. Over the years, we have traveled so many roads together with hills and valleys, mountains and canyons. Among our travels, we have always been there for each other. Our "tangled web" has made us closer and stronger with each passing day. Very few people find a true best friend in another, but I must be one of the lucky ones. I could not have done this without you.

Acknowledgement must also be given to the countless medical professionals, technicians, nurses, therapists, doctors, practitioners, lab workers, etc., for their respective expertise in my treatment. Special appreciation is given to Dr. B, my primary care physician, Dr. D, my gynecologist, Dr. Q, my surgical oncologist and his nurse, Diane, Dr. E., my medical oncologist, her nurse practitioner, Beth, and nurse, Sharon as well as Dr. C., my radiation oncologist. This team of <u>brilliant</u> doctors and nurses made the seemingly impossible, possible. For many more years to come, I will now live a full and healthy life, thanks to their dedication and expertise. Consequently, much of the proceeds from this book will be donated to continue the vital breast cancer research at UMASS Hospital in Worcester, Massachusetts. Forever, I am thankful, as is Dennis and Bryce.

I also am indebted and inspired by yet more family, friends and colleagues who helped to make the lows bearable and the highs exceptional in this great roller coaster. Thank you to ...

- Jessica, my cousin, for pointing out the "good things" – lack of gray hairs, the thought of me as a curly blonde and great boobs at the outset of this situation. Your thoughts made me laugh early on when laughter was sparse.
- Jessica, my friend and colleague, who gave me a meditation DVD, which I used faithfully each day of recovery. And likewise, to my friend, Diana who shared her favorite meditations with me while also enjoying a movie night and cup of tea with me.
- Lizzibean, who entertained me with delicious dinners, movie-dates, phone calls and sound advice. Thank you for being so strong. And to her husband, Andrew, who educated me on the "ins and outs" of anesthesia during surgery – this was more appreciated than you can imagine.
- My friends, Megan and Kot, for making me laugh daily, for hot chocolate, excellent advice and endearing support. You are both incredible.
- Bethany, my friend, who read health books with me so as to figure out the next stages in my recovery.

- My friend Shauna, who always knew what to do at the perfect time: babysitting, special treats in the mail, enriching conversations. I love you.
- Brenda (aka Mimi), who is a best friend to me: nurturing and loving; she always knew how to make things right – the English way, of course.
- My friends, Sarah S., Sarah and Dave M. and Maryann for being constant sources of support, encouragement and love. I could not have traveled day by day without each of you by my side.
- Melissa, my friend and colleague, who helped me with my caseload during my recovery and who was always up for dinner and laughs.
- Dennis, Shauna, Megan and Kot for helping me decide on a title for this memoir and reviewing the cover proposal.
- Cam, Bryce's first schoolteacher, who helped us maintain routine and development during a seemingly chaotic time. Cam – you are truly amazing, and we love you.
- Maryellen and Lynn, who gave me inspiration in knowing that there was a happy ending to be had.
- My good friend, Aixa, for believing in me and sharing literature and resources that aided in my healing.
- Miss Julie and the moms at music class for livening my Monday mornings.

- Nancy E. from LS, especially, for allowing my husband the time he needed while also supporting us fully and being there, always. We are both blessed to have her in our lives.
- My students and parents, who were flexible, understanding, caring and empathetic. I will forever be grateful.
- Whitney, who always wears a smile and makes the most heartfelt gifts.
- My work colleagues, who brought meals, sent cards and gift baskets, who stood by my every decision, who were flexible and understanding, who made me laugh and who provided a housekeeper for me. This group of professionals and friends are a blessing to Dennis, Bryce and me. The ease at which I journeyed through the year would not have been so if the ongoing love and support from my school "family" had not been there. And on a lighter note, so many of my work colleagues were extremely generous as to suggest the donation of their extra adipose tissue to my eventual augmentation. Ha, ha!
- Nana Arpi and Grandma Margie whom I miss daily. They would have been proud of me.
- All the other family and friends who supported me in ways both big and small; I could write another book solely for these folks. Everything said, done or given to me has made all the difference. Thank you.

In adversity keep motivated, for often the best comes from difficulty.

-   Norman Vincent Peale

Voice of Optimism
- Lisa Phillips

Hello Everyone,

This email will be a surprise for most while some of you may already know. I have been trying to contact everyone personally, but it is getting difficult. I hope you can understand. Well, I have been diagnosed with breast cancer. This completely sucks, but I am going to be very positive throughout this process and need everyone around me to be happy, funny and positive too. To keep all updated with my success in treatment, Dennis, my husband, created a blog. I am going to try my best to keep it going, as I think it will be very therapeutic for me. Please comment on the site and spread it around. I will look forward to even the smallest of chats. And of course, I will talk with you all soon, but I wanted you to hear this from me first and not through the grapevine. I love you all, and we will get through this mess.

Love,
Lisa

A good friend of mine ends every email with "onward and upward," and how this echoes for me now. So I have been diagnosed with the ever-feared C. Regardless, I am going to kick this and live my life for a LONG time. This blog is for readers to hear my story, comment positive thoughts, funny thoughts and uplifting thoughts. No sappy sadness here – it is NOT allowed. I will also let my friends and family know what I might need and how I am moving along so that you can help in ways I need help. My sincerest thanks in advance for everything and lots of love, always! SMILE!

- Lisa Phillips

Prologue

This memoir was initially written with no expectation other than to journal my experiences to inform family and friends of my treatment regime. Over the months however, many approached me with remarks about how my strength was an inspiration to them. My response was always, "I don't know how to do this any differently other than to be positive." Leading up to my diagnosis, I encountered three different doctors that suggested what I was feeling was nothing other than a cyst. It was not until Dr. D, my gynecologist, decided to be thorough and follow-up on my concerns with a mammogram and ultrasound. As it turned out, I did in fact have cancer below the cyst I felt.

You know, everything happens for a reason. Right before I was diagnosed, I miscarried. Though devastated at the time, I realize now that without her, my guardian angel, I may not have found the cyst. This cyst is what eventually prompted the diagnostic procedures that imaged my breast cancer. Everything in life is truly a blessing; I have learned this over the course of my recovery. I hope that through my writing, I can help others in ways that so many have helped me. Whether you or a loved one is going through breast cancer, it is reassuring to know that there are others, and many of us, who have had uplifting success stories in surviving breast cancer.

So Far

I smile every time I look at my son, Bryce. He is completely adorable. I have to see him grow into a fine young man with his own family and children because he is amazing. This is my goal. I am staying positive and RELAXED, which is hard for me. Honestly I am scared out of my mind, but have to keep focused and positive. This is going to be my mantra for the next year in order to get through this journey.

The cancer is in the right breast, mostly contained within the ducts. Doctors are encouraged because there are no large tumors, though the cancer did proceed to the right lymph node(s). The biopsy indicated invasive cancer in at least one node and likely four in total. Only one was biopsied, and here I am. As I write this, my story becomes more real. I am 31 for goodness sake, but this will be to my advantage. I have to believe that. My surgical oncologist is outstanding, and I meet with the whole team of specialists on Wednesday. Dennis, my husband, has been there every step of the way, and my family and friends have been terrific, too.

The support, company, relaxation techniques, yoga DVDs, funny, positive stories and uplifting thoughts are the perfect remedies to combat the obvious stressors of my diagnosis. For example, my cousin Jess called this evening and said, "Well Lisa, I have been thinking all day about the good things of this. I came up with three – (1) you won't have grays when your hair grows back after chemo, (2) you could come back as a curly blonde and (3) you will have awesome boobs when they reconstruct them..." I realize the road will be a rough one, but the power of positive thinking is going to get my though this mess.

Feeling Good Today

Bryce is such a ham. He is always smiling, which is so refreshing. This morning, he cuddled with me before coming downstairs for French toast sticks and a "lil- bit" of his favorite movie. All is good so far. I have an appetite; my nerves have settled, and I am looking forward to Wednesday when I can begin the process of putting this behind me. My positive energy must be attributed to a "lil bit" of my favorite movie, meditation before bed and sour peach rings – yum! Already, I have had really positive stories shared with me, and I love it. This morning, I learned of a friend whose husband survived breast cancer.

Roller Coaster

When I was little, I remember going on my very first roller coaster ride with dad. I believe it was the large white corkscrew at old Rocky Point Park in Rhode Island. Vividly, I recall being at the top of a gigantic upside down loop and asking, "Dad, can we go back? I can't do this" (or something along those lines if my memory serves me right). He laughed and replied, "Yes you can; no turning back now." I never thought that memory would get me through this journey today. And the end result – I love roller coasters and have a joyous feeling when the ride is over. The same sensation will also surface at the end of this "ride." Of course when this ride is over, I am not purchasing tickets for another round.

Today, I had an MRI. By far, an MRI provides the loudest banging into the eardrums – a potential correlation for early hearing loss? Nevertheless, as I listened to commercials about a local state college and songs reminiscent of my college days, I had a solid forty-five minutes to reflect on the upcoming year. Conclusion: my road to recovery is starting now. I also realize that I can sleep through anything – what banging!

You Can Drink Anything

Today was relatively uneventful, thankfully. A lot of tests. The morning began with a CT scan of my chest and abdomen area. Those blessed with not having had a CT scan before are also lucky to have avoided drinking the 32 oz. barium concoction required of this procedure. But as my husband always says to me, "you can drink anything!" I was up for the challenge, and I quickly guzzled the potion while the guy in the next chair nursed it more slowly. Honestly, I was envisioning a mudslide. Afterwards, the time came to scan my bones. Prior to the scan, the technologist injected me with a radioactive die to better assess my bone mass on imaging. That scan was about twenty minutes long, and I slept (again, confirming that I can sleep through nearly everything). Doc said my bones were "beautiful." Well, that is encouraging. Later on while driving home, a bird pooped on my car – good luck, right? Positive signs today! I'll take them. After a day of scans completed, I arranged my cape and flew off to tutor.

Skinny Waist and Big Boobs

At 9:00 this morning, the revolving door of specialists began – surgical oncologist, medical oncologist, radiation oncologist, plastic surgeon, health psychologist, nurse practitioner, a few fellows, a few nurses and a partridge in a pear tree. As it turns out, these intelligent men and women shared the exciting news that my cancer remains in the right breast and lymph. All of my scans and MRI were clean showing no spread elsewhere. THIS IS GREAT! I have what the docs consider Stage II cancer, and it is very treatable. Chemo starts next Wednesday for a total of 6 infusions spread over 5 months. After that, I will have a bilateral mastectomy, radiation and delayed reconstruction.

Skinny waist and BIG Boobs?! By way of reconstruction, the plastic surgeon will take fat from my belly, wave his magic scalpel and transform the fat into perky boobs. "Bibbidi, bobbidi, boo!" Impressive. That is a while away of course so in the interim, cheers to a new Lisa. I plan to donate my hair to "locks of love," which means I will to have to chop it rather short in the next week or two. On

Monday, I intend to look at some wigs and on Wednesday, the first infusion of chemotherapy will take place. Quite a lot at once, but I am looking forward to checking this off one of many life accomplishments.

Sometime in the midst of all my appointments today, I learned of an organization that makes "Jacki's" for women who have had mastectomy. These jackets help with drainage, and are given to patients at no cost to make recovery marginally easier. I have the sporty version of the "Jacki" that I plan to wear proudly and set this year's new fashion trend. Just as Bryce says, "me share with you..," I too will let anyone that is interested borrow this overwhelmingly cool attire on occasion.

Pencils Come from Pennsylvania

What a refreshing change of pace and return to some semblance of normality. Rather than conversing with gifted and talented physicians, I was instead surrounded by loving and warm friends at work. I feel overwhelmingly grateful for everyone's concern and positive energy. My day was filled with laughs, smiles, *interesting* discussions around, well, I think I

will restrain from continuing my thoughts
here, and a visit with a local meteorologist.
Mr. B., the meteorologist, came to my place of
employment, and it was quite exciting. Of
course I inquired, "How's the weather?"
Okay that is a bit cliché, but anyway... As the
day marched on, I went about my merry way
through the bright halls of the Elementary
School where I work, when I overheard a
student remark, "yes, pencils come from
Pennsylvania." Oh children say the darnedest
things! I chuckled quietly as I was also
reminded of my own childhood when I
somehow believed peanuts came from
elephants. No comments from the "peanut"
gallery!

I must close now and fit in some moderate
exercise. Have to prepare for my heart test
tomorrow as well as for a string of other
doctors including a geneticist.

Thought of the Day: Eat an apple daily (with
the skin); I hear it does wonders for your
health. And, what is "tea tree" oil? My
oncologist suggested I use this for my hands
and nails.

You Can Do This for Me, Mommy

The events of today centered around visits
with the geneticist and cardiologist in the

morning and an ultrasound this evening. The cardiologist called my heart "textbook perfect." Fabulous! Therefore, I am ready to undergo chemo this Wednesday and excited to start my recovery. Later on, I met the geneticist, and we mapped out my family tree to possibly find the roots of this conundrum in which I now find myself. The day proceeded rather typically after these morning appointments with play, naptime and mommy duty until about 4:00 when homemade organic lasagna arrived at my doorstep from a dear work friend. I could really get used to these meals on wheels. The royal treatment continued when Bryce and my mom gave me a sweet foot and leg massage before returning to UMASS for an evening ultrasound. Jen, my future sister-in-law, came along for the ride, and we found ourselves locked in a hospital stairwell. By use of our problem solving skills, we finally arrived for the ultrasound. After drinking 32 ounces of water without going potty, I thought my bladder would explode. Fortunately, I was the next appointment. On route home, I picked up a gigantic Minnie balloon for Bryce, gave him lots of hugs and kisses, read him books and smiled when he said, "you can do this for me, mommy."

Aglets

This morning I went for a hot stone massage–
definitely the highlight of my day.
Afterwards, I returned home, relaxed with
Dennis, ventured off to the gym and caught
up on some reading. A friend Diana loaned
me one of her favorite health books. I learned
that restricting calories, increasing strength
and getting quality sleep are three of nature's
best medicines for living a long, healthy life.
And even more interesting – if a good habit is
maintained for three years, the effect on
one's body is as significant as if this positive
habit had been done for one's entire life.
There were so many interesting factoids, (i.e.
"aglets.") Aglets are the little plastic tips on
shoelaces. The writer was using aglets as a
metaphor for telomeres, essential building
blocks for cell growth. Hmm...

Inspired By Fish

To be *inspired* by fish is a first secondary to
my perpetual and ever-growing *fear* of fish!
No really, I am petrified! Why? Perhaps an
early childhood scar? Who knows? This
irrational fear has become a bit of a mockery
in recent years, certainly amplified by my
behaviors. For instance this summer at the
beach, I made a point to holler out to anyone

who would listen, "Are there any fish out there?" Definitely something to laugh about! In fact, I am laughing aloud as I write while Dennis is probably questioning my sanity.

Speaking of fish, I must have *inadvertently* forgotten to mention that Bryce now has two lovely goldfish – aptly named, Nemo and Dory. Since going to a Disney on Ice Performance with Uncle Eddy and Aunty Jen, Bryce has developed a recent affinity for fish. In retrospect, my adage that everything happens for a reason holds true once again. During the performance, the always optimistic and loving Dory sings "just keep swimming, just keep swimming..." and this melody reverberates loudly for me these days. Like Dory, I too will "just keeping swimming, just keep swimming..." And even better, I have a visual reminder of our Nemo and Dory each morning when Bryce and I feed them two flakes of food. Tomorrow is "wig-fitting day." Hmm, should I go a shade of blonde or maybe, pink? Decisions. Decisions.

Strike a Pose

The *highlight* of today was my adventure
with Dad, my brother, Eddy, and Jen to the
salon for a new hairstyle. I promptly arrived
at the Image Center in Leominster to meet
the divine Mary who will take care of the bald
factor. After trying on an assortment of wigs
– blonde, "old lady like," brunette, short and
long, Bryce, my partner in crime and biggest
fan, decided on a short "bob" style to
perfectly compliment my olive-toned skin
and brown eyes. While this wig is natural
looking, it will be strange to have perfectly
styled hair all the time. I found myself
flashing back to the days when high school
pals called me "Pantene Payne," my maiden
name. In addition to the above-described
wig, I chose a second equally perfect one to
use at the gym and around the house. The
second wig is quite deceiving in that there is
no top, only elastics to keep it securely in

place. Therefore, a bandana or hat is necessary to cover the top of my head. The half-wig is perfect for the gym: my head can breath, and I won't damage the better accessory. Following an exciting hour of striking a pose for my entourage, I was then explicitly instructed in ten cardinal rules of wig care.

1. Store wig on an upside down vase to preserve its shape.

2. Wash with color-treated shampoo and conditioner after every 7 wears. So in between, does the hair get oily? Pretty low maintenance.

3. Let hair dry over night.

4. Comb only when dry.

5. Never use a curling iron.

6. Never use a straightener.

7. Never wear in kitchen for fear of it igniting over Mac n' cheese preparation.

8. If the wig is tangled and begins to look like a wild cat, treat it with the same tender, love and care that you would a

gnarled cat - one tangle at a time.

9. Stay clear of ethnic restaurants and campfires unless these aromas are deemed desirable fragrances.

10. No profuse sweating when wearing the wig. Guess I will have to tone down my Wii Fit workouts.

The Road Less Traveled

Today when driving to work, I found myself drifting in and out of thoughts. Of course, this is hazardous considering I should have been paying closer attention to the snowy roadway. However, it was the picturesque scenery that put me into this hypnotic trance. Anyway as I continued along to work, I reflected about living in the day and transposed myself into scenes from a familiar poem. The road I am traveling these days is certainly less frequented by most 31-year olds; however, it has truly made "all the difference" in my life. Blessed by this experience, I have grown closer to friends, family, and work colleagues as well as inspired by touching stories and intrigued by medical professionals who have taken stellar care of me. A little sentimental I know, but it was on my mind.

Once again, my sentiments were peppered with laughter throughout the day when one of my colleagues, and friend, brought in booby cupcakes to an afternoon meeting. Very funny, if I must say so myself! Some nipples were perky, others inverted. This act spurred interesting conversation.

First Day of Chemotherapy

In my spare time today, I read of a woman who summed up being a friend of someone going through cancer. She wrote along the lines of, *"Hi, my name is ... I'm a sucking black hole of emotional need right now. My hobbies are taking drugs, napping and calling people I hardly know for emergency child-care. Wanna be my friend?"* While I am not a "sucking black hole of emotional need," I still found humor in this quote.

The long-awaited details of my first day of treatment follow. In the same amount of time I succumbed to the "chemo chair," I could have flown to Switzerland and Venice – two of my favorite vacation destinations. Dennis and I arrived this morning with an edible arrangement for all my new friends, saviors at the Comprehensive Breast Center in Massachusetts. We were then whisked away to the third floor where oncologists met with me, took vitals and reexamined my deflated, bruised breasts for any palpable changes. The fun, and I do mean this sincerely in that it is *fun* to get better, continued when I was escorted to my cubicle of chemo. It was here that I met my oncologist nurse – a truly lovely and empathetic woman who also survived breast cancer. She arranged all the IVs and lines to initiate treatment. At the time of my writing, I feel loopy from Ativan and find it difficult to process what I long to say. But here's to an authentic blog! It is 4:34, and Dennis seems uncomfortable by the looks of his positioning in the chair next to me though he still sleeps. In the mean time, I am soaking up the final installment of a three-part mixture of drugs. What Dennis and I found most unexpected about today was the sheer length of treatment. Each infusion will be four to five hours long taking place on Thursdays, every three weeks, with the next one in middle of February. I decided that after every round of chemotherapy, I will treat myself to something new. The first purchase will occur this weekend – a stair master or eclipse machine. Even though I have been told by Dennis' friends to eat lots of hamburgers for bigger boobs, it seems in my better interest to remain healthy. Today more than ever, I also realize how important Dennis is and will be to keep me strong throughout. Truly, he is the most remarkable, loving, caring husband and father, and Bryce and I love and need him so much. By default, he too is surviving cancer. He deserves to be pampered.

Locks of Love

I cut my hair off, and there will not be a picture taken because I absolutely detest it. The haircut is fine, but it is just not Lisa. I haven't had my hair this short since my 2nd grade bowl cut. Having said that, I started wearing my "half-wig" today. I like it and feel comfortable sporting this new style. I have also found bandanas to be a fun fashion accessory. In the meantime, I sent my flowing long brown locks off to locks of love: two 10-inch ponytails. That was the highlight of my day. Feeling great thus far: no nausea, good appetite and energy. The power of positive thinking all the way, baby! A friend came over to visit tonight so she was, by default, the guinea pig of my new "do," and it went over well.

Me!

Today for the first time in several days, I am tongue-tied. Strange, considering I am a "talking therapist," as Dennis so aptly describes my profession. Nonetheless, my state of *ankyloglossia* cannot last long around my house as Bryce is a driving force of constant inspiration and love – an instant fix for writer's block. Therefore as I began to write this evening I asked Bryce, "Beebs, what should Mommy write about in her journal." Just as I would expect, Bryce replied gregariously, "ME!!!" He always makes me laugh, though I have to work on his articulation these days. Nemo being "-uckin' fish tank" instead of *stuck in the fish tank* is spurring some curious looks from strangers.

Anyway, kudos to another great day of energy, spirit and positive vibes! My mom, dad and I hung out with Bryce for the majority of the afternoon. Then later on, I went to pick up my wig. While at the salon, I asked Bryce if he too would like a wig. He candidly responded, "No mama, I already have hair." With all these new hairpieces, I could certainly provide, quite variably, some eccentric Halloween costumes to interested parties. My brother has already placed dibs.

Yucky Muscles

You can find laughter in just about any situation. Today, my achy muscles and joints made their way to Sears to look at elliptical machines. On route, my boys and I were chatting when Bryce said, "Mom, you have yucky muscles." Poetic, considering our intended shopping adventure. Dennis and I laughed and laughed, truly the best therapy as well as the makings of a joyous car ride. Although we did not come home with an elliptical machine tonight, the first chemo purchase will be soon. Dennis already splurged on a pair of Air Jordan's, so I have to catch up.

Nothing Worth Doing is Easy

While I continue to maintain happy spirits, and excitement that I am a day closer to recovery, I will admit that this morning was a bit jagged around the edges. As my achy muscles relaxed some, the stomach juices were triggered. Fortunately, my darling hubby was home so I could sleep off these ailments. In the midst of my un-pleasantries, Dennis stood by me the whole time and reiterated that, "nothing worth doing is easy."

How true!

After winning the "family sleeping contest," I bathed Bryce, read him a dozen books or so and put him to sweet dreams while Dennis went grocery shopping, cleaned the kitchen and folded the laundry. Another eventful day in the Phillips' Saga, which will continue in the morning.

Mama, Your Hair Fell Off?

A healthy day today: no nausea, no fever. Woo hoo! I am also blessed with family and friends, who take time out of their already busy schedules to see me, write me and simply, check-in. I could not do this otherwise.

So today, I thought I would get used to wearing my stylish wig since tomorrow, I return to work with this new look. As I fiddled about trying to get the side tabs and back pull all lined up to correctly place my new hair accessory, Bryce watched in wonderment. Candidly as always, he questioned, "Mama, your hair fell off?" That is an understatement if I've ever heard one. Anyway, the wig placement finally worked, and as I walked into the kitchen to get Beebs breakfast, one of the ten cardinal rules reverberated soundly in my head. "Never wear in kitchen for fear of it igniting over Mac n' Cheese preparation." Although I was not fixing Mac n' Cheese, I figured the same principles would apply to pancakes and bacon. Therefore, off went the wig.

Round 2 – This time, I thought I would try putting a net underneath the wig to place it more securely. Bryce loves to tug at my hair, and I envisioned a flying toupee across music class. The net placement did not work so well, and the wig shifted so much backward now that both the hairline and net were revealed. When I went to adjust the wig, the damn thing popped off my head.

Round 3 – Finally, I figured out the mechanics of wig placement. Who would have thought such complexities would occur before 9:00 am? All said and done, Bryce, Aunt Donna and I gallivanted off to music class to join in singing, "Hello everybody so glad to see you..." and well, I won't get carried away with lyrics. And thankfully, you cannot hear my "luminous" voice as you read. Following music class, we three musketeers retreated back home for lunch and an afternoon siesta. You know, Europeans have the sleep-wake cycle all figured out. Siestas rock! The day continued as normal and was topped off with an edible arrangement delivered to my door. Hit the spot!

Day One: Synthetic Locks

I have the most wonderful life: an incredible husband and son, family, friends, work colleagues and students. I am truly blessed by support, understanding and love everywhere I go. A glistening tear. Amazing, really!

I made it through a full day at work while also sporting the synthetic brown locks. I found humor in the fact that a few staff members and all students thought my new style was simply the result of a different haircut – if they only know what lied beneath. While no one will ever see what lies beneath, I have to confess a few times throughout the day, I was tempted to whip it off. Maybe tomorrow. After work, I rested to expend a final burst of energy on my new cross trainer. The first chemo purchase was successfully made. Hmmm, what will be next?

It's Not the Hand that Feeds You; It's the Heart that Beats for You.

Today was an exceptional day for me, truly inspirational. And, it all began with a nosebleed. On the way to work this morning, Bryce and I were gleefully singing along when suddenly I felt a "colorful" sneeze come on. Who knew that sneezing would trigger an unforeseen nosebleed in the middle of our previously joyous ride to school? Fortunately, I was well equipped with my trusty first aid kit and quickly grabbed some gauze and wipes to clean up my now red polka-dotted vehicle. Situation under control! Bryce at school. Mom at work. All is good ... until round two. This time, I was in the middle of a lesson when Niagara Falls started. Damn it! I quickly made my way to the school nurse, snatched more gauze, held the bridge of my nose like I used to in my earlier days of incessant nose bleeds, and camped out in a colleague's office for a solid fifteen minutes until the flood again subsided. It was here that a met a most wonderful woman who took me under her wing by sharing her tale of surviving breast cancer. She too was a young woman, like me, when diagnosed and continues to live strong and well. Later in the evening, I had another chance to speak with her and was inspired by her story, by her courage. When describing her will to be there for her family she spoke volumes with "it's not the hand that feeds you, it's the heart that beats for you." My heart beats so strong for my son, my husband and my family. And it is this, which will conquer all.

Health and Energy

Wow, I am on a good streak. Another healthy and energetic day! In the spirit of well being, I thought to try something new – cooking. Over the weekend, I will try a Millet and Swiss Chard Casserole. I read that Millet can be quite tasty, and like everything else these days, I am expanding my horizon. Although "cooking and cleaning" typically go hand and hand, the cleaning will have to wait. The tornado that blew through my downstairs is a bitch of a storm, and the debris is just way too much to tackle this evening. Hey, Rome was not built in a day. As I have learned, there are *many* more important things to focus attention. For example, singing! On a ride back from Athens Pizza tonight, Dennis and I bellowed "heeey-hey-hey-hey-hey-heyyy" from a popular top-40-song. It was fun and random, and even more amusing when Bryce stared at his completely insane parents bug-eyed and entranced. Though for being two and a half years old, he is quite savvy. Bryce's "wassup" addition to the song added more humor to this already delirious situation. The rest of the evening proceeded as normal except for my crazy cat springing to a door handle in attempt to escape the confines of our bedroom. No wait, she is always crazy so this behavior is quite normal!

My writing closes today with a countdown to hair loss – 6 days to go. So far, I have lost 8 strands. Yes, I am counting. My head itches like the markings of poison ivy or sumac. Dennis is convinced I will be the 1-2% of people that do not lose hair. We will see in due time.

Laugh

Bryce, my friend Liz, and I went to see a children's movie at the local theater. "See" is an operative word here in that I <u>could</u> <u>not</u> do so effectively. Presenting as extremely near-sighted, which is not typically the case, I phoned my doctor. Turns out that one of the nausea meds was negatively influencing my vision. Solution: Discontinue use of that medication, and vision will soon return. That aside, later on, I spontaneously burst out into laughter (an experiment of sorts). Bryce's expression transitioned from confusion to grins to smiles and then he too started laughing hysterically. The two of us roared for a straight five minutes and I felt like I was walking on air. So here is a challenge – Laugh! Laugh a straight five minutes for no reason other than to laugh and have fun. Laughter is the best therapy.

Well, off to purchase the ingredients for Millet and Swiss Chard Casserole. A point of reference – millet is a whole grain, not a fish. I am petrified of fish; that would be a torturous "horizon expansion" for me. Speaking of fish, Kacey, my cat, is now tapping at Nemo and Dory. More than ever, they better "just keep swimming."

Lisa's Top Ten

Yesterday I read that finding joy in cancer is challenging. And while I would not wish this *bump* in the road on myself nor anyone else, somehow, my optimism perseveres through it all. So here are the top ten reasons, in no particular order, for smiling toward recovery.

1. Daily sentiments and thoughts from family and friends.

2. A no-nonsense hairdo everyday of the week.

3. Edible arrangements.

4. Fresh bouquets of flowers.

5. An array of gifts, consistently.

6. Home-cooked, prepared meals.

7. Free housekeeping – http://www.cleaningforareason.com

8. Free massages – http://www.healinggarden.net/

9. An automatic excuse to relax whenever needed.

10. A free boob job and tummy tuck at the outset.

See, not so bad!   Had fun in RI today celebrating my brother's 28th birthday. As I write this, my nose started bleeding – Grrrrr! Until tomorrow...

Do You Sell Millet?

While feeling energetic and strong, Bryce and I made an outing to a handful of local grocery stores in search of millet. By far, this is the hardest whole grain to acquire. After touring the nearby stores, a phone call to the Whole Foods market was all it took to solve the mystery of where to find millet. Though in my jaunt around town, I did buy a package of millet flour. I can now whip up a fabulous batch of pumpkin cookies for anyone interested, but the Millet and Swiss Chard Casserole will have to wait.

Other than that, my high was Bryce spontaneously reiterating, "I love you mom" during dinner while my *low* was falling off the Wii Fit balance board during the "Rhythm Parade." Ha, ha! A famous doctor writes that laughter "increases natural killer cells that destroy tumors and viruses." Considering how often I laugh when writing my own blogs, lame, I know, as well as during today's feeble attempt to march on a board without tumbling off, I am well on my way to beating this thing. Even more hilarious is the fact that I was a majorette captain in high school. Marching is the default mechanism for success as a majorette. (Sigh) Count down to hair loss – 3 days.

Sentiment from a Student

While the truck responsible for delivery of my new cross trainer broke down on route to our home, it remained a splendid day characterized by contagious laughs, playful songs at music class, great company and plentiful smiles. The revised delivery time for our cross trainer is late tomorrow. Woo hoo!!   Perhaps this mishap is really a sign to try "Rhythm Parade," yet again.

Today, I was deeply touched by one of my students. She is an endearing and lovely young lady who took the time to make a jewelry box, necklace, ring, bracelet and pair of earrings for me. On the jewelry box, she engraved "ar," which is a sound we have been practicing. I will treasure her sentiment, always.

I like to write in the evening to summarize the whole day's events. As I write this – no, I do not have a nosebleed, I casually run my fingers through my unpleasantly short hair to extract four strands simultaneously. I actually felt them uproot from my scalp – weird!

It is time. I decided that Dennis is buzzing my hair when he returns from the gym. I am taking control.

Whatever You Do is What Shall Be

Last night, Dennis came home from the gym, and I confidently declared, "let's buzz my hair." Though I have to admit, I chickened out. Instead, I chopped locks off the top with my trusty scissors. It was exhilarating to give myself a haircut, and I would be more than willing to share my new expertise with any brave, and I do mean brave, volunteers. It is the new style – very Sinead O'Connor with a touch of auburn. The only thing more bizarre would possibly be if I broke out into chanting from my heart, like the actress from a recent Hollywood film I saw: "...to the window, to the walls ...woooo woooo...let me see you get low....stop, wiggle it, just jiggle it..."

Okay, I admit I am engrossed in this particular movie, absolutely love it, and I have rewound that part five times. I also adore another beloved actress in this same movie. Soon after the chanting in the woods subsides, she shares a bit of wisdom in saying, "whatever you do is what shall be."

I shall be strong. I shall be affectionate and loving. I shall be the best I can be, always!

On an unrelated note, my cross trainer arrived.

Superwoman

Recently, I came across a quote that read, "It has been said that we take on the strength of that which we overcome." At the outset of this debacle, I plan to be superwoman. These days, I require lots of daily strength, which I receive from my supportive husband and son, family and friends, my writing, books I read and laughter. With each passing day, I feel stronger physically and mentally. Today, my work friends set up the most amazing resource to bring meals to my house on Mondays, Wednesdays and Fridays. Dennis and I are thrilled about this generosity in that he does not have to cook nearly as frequently, and my wig won't ignite over French toast or Mac n' Cheese preparation.

Before I dive into bath time with Bryce, I have a baldness joke to share. Did you know that baldness is a sign of intelligence? Read on. Little Billy is eating breakfast one morning and gets to thinking about things. Mommy, mommy, why does Bald Bill have so few hairs

on his head?" he asks his mother. He thinks a
lot," replies his mother, pleased with herself
for coming up with such a quick answer to
Little Billy's question. Or she was, until Billy
thinks for a second and asks, "So why do you
have so much hair?"

A Hair Day is a Good Day

Losing hair is an anomaly I cannot quite wrap
my mind around. As I run my fingers over
my follically challenged roots, strands just let
go into my hand. Weird! Regardless of this
seemingly devastating side effect, it was
actually quite amusing earlier today. I
attended a conference on reading and
dyslexia, which was not as appealing as the
brochure promised. Anyway, in the midst of
my attention (or inattention) to the speaker,
the strands falling from my scalp mesmerized
me. Evidently, they were bored too. I
counted a total of thirty-four – even lined
them up on the table. Okay, that last part was
an exaggeration, but the thought crossed my
mind. I read that you have to lose 50% of
your hair before it is noticeable to others; I
wonder when that will be. Though, just as
my short hair is not up for demonstration,
neither will my bald head.

Today, my inquisitive Bryce questioned, "Mama, your hair fall out?" It was extremely cute; a curious soul is he. I replied, "Yes, isn't that silly?" to which he retorted "Yah!" The love of a child through all of this has been amazing.

Closing my writing today with a few jokes that struck my funny bone:

1. Science has found that only one thing can prevent baldness ... hair!

2. What did the bald woman say when she got a comb for her birthday? Thanks, I'll never part with it.

Millet and Swiss Chard Casserole

I did it! I made Millet and Swiss Chard Casserole, also known as birdseed in a dish, and Dennis ate the whole thing up. He couldn't get enough, definitely his new favorite. In actuality, Millet and Swiss Chard is interesting to say the least – kind of bland, but very healthy. Although I should probably give millet a rest, the next dish will be Millet Chili. At the outset of this snafu, I am hosting a "Nut and Millet" cancer-free party. Menu will include an assortment of nuts - almonds, walnuts, Brazil nuts to start. The main course will include a choice of Millet and Swiss Chard Casserole or Millet Chili. Following the main entree, you may choose either dark chocolate millet-dipped strawberries or broiled mango.

Beyond the making of this fine dish, I had an enjoyable and strong day. My mom came to visit, and we spent most of the afternoon in a tranquil retreat of sorts, nature trails and waterfalls. A perfect day!

Pre-Valentine's Celebration

It all started with a lovely evening, a pre-Valentine's Day celebration with my dear hubby. I was whisked away to fine dining, exquisite dessert, then endless laughter at the movies. While the evening seemed perfect, life would not be such without its twists and turns. Rewind to 5:50 this evening. Simultaneous with our being seated at our favorite steak house in New Hampshire, we both received a phone call that followed.

"This is ADT Security Service leaving a message for Lisa Phillips. We are receiving a burglar alarm from your home. This number is on the contact list provided. We have already notified the police. If you have any questions, please contact ADT."

WHAT??!! Any questions? Of course, we have questions. In the midst of our fine dining, all was put on hold to contact ADT. We learned that the living room sensor went off, and we couldn't imagine why. Did Kacey have a burst of energy, spring four feet into the air and trigger the alarm? So Pete and Dave, both "key holders" and friends in the area, were summoned by the local Police Department for further examination of the property.

Rewind 3 days ago ...

Dennis: Do you think we can get rid of this stupid gigantic Minnie Mouse balloon?

Lisa: No, I like it.

Rewind 2 days ago ...

Dennis: Do you think we can get rid of this stupid gigantic Minnie Mouse balloon?

Lisa: No, I like it.

<u>Rewind to yesterday ...</u>

Dennis: Do you think we can get rid of this stupid gigantic Minnie Mouse balloon?

Lisa: No, I like it.

So as it turns out, the 4-foot tall "stupid gigantic Minnie Mouse balloon," which I bought for my son a little over three weeks ago, was the *intruder* that prompted the call from ADT. The rest, as they say, is history. Speaking of history, Nemo, our fish, kicked the bucket.

You Almost Look Like Dad

This morning I ventured off to a tapestry class, hoping for tranquility after last night's excitement with the cops. To my utter disappointment, it was more of a "mope-fest, woe is me; I have Cancer" group of ladies that I could not relate with on any other level than our sharing of this diagnosis. While these women were quite nice, the group was not a healthy fit for me. Therefore, I bee-lined out of there, chatted with friends on the phone, listened to music and proceeded with my day.

 Let's fast forward to bath, books and bedtime when I was brushing Bryce's teeth to keep away the "yucky bugs," as I refer to plaque. During this routine, one of his favorite past-times is to hug me tightly, grasping onto my hair and holding tight. Well I'm sure you can guess where this is going. With his final release, out came a "hair bunch" to which Bryce replied "uh oh..." We realized the time to buzz was now, unless of course, I was to sport a rather large bald spot on the back of my head. So out came the buzzers, and my boys buzzed off my hair, which cascaded gently to the kitchen floor with grace and beauty. Throughout the process Bryce exclaimed repeatedly, "Almost there, you almost look like dad." Honestly, he is so cute. Along this road, Bryce remains unscathed.

Patches of Hair

"You look silly," comments Bryce on my new "hair," or lack thereof. Ah, the honesty of a child. He hit the nail right on the head. My situation grossly reminds me of children's book, Mrs. Honey's Hat by Pam Adams. In the story, "Mrs. Honey had a very busy week. She went out every day, wearing her best hat. She especially liked the decorations but so did everybody else. What a surprise Mrs. Honey had at the end of the week when she looked at herself in the mirror!" Mrs. Honey was surprised by the inevitable mess of her hat with bubble gum and a bird's nest in lieu of dainty bows and flowers. My surprise at the end of the week was in the patches of baldness all over my scalp after my hair was buzzed. Regardless, I have found definite benefits to having limited amounts of hair, so cheers to all my bald or balding friends and loving husband. In no particular order, here are the top five reasons that alopecia can be a good thing.

1. You save $ on shampoo and conditioner as well as other hair products for that matter.

2. There is not one tangle to speak of.

3. During the summer months, it will facilitate complete coolness – temperature <u>and</u> style.

4. You can hop out of bed, brush your teeth and head out for the day. No styling required! By far, it is the most low maintenance haircut.

5. You will never have hat head.

Shooting Water

Two more days until chemotherapy. I am thrilled because I am so much closer to a full recovery. The events of today included more hair loss, now resembling the skin of a leopard – patches of nude-colored scalp and brown buzzed hair. Quite amusing, though surprisingly, I like my scalp. In addition to diminishing hair, I was also blessed with a unexpected half day at work, an enjoyable afternoon lounging with my boys and shooting water during our tax preparation in the evening. As we were reviewing numbers with our tax guy, Joe, I felt a sudden urge for some water. I meandered my way down the hall to find a bubbler and *attempted* to get a drink – only to find a geyser ready to explode. I nearly fell over on my first attempt by the force of the shooting water. Oh, but it gets better. As I am a determined person, I tried once again, (and a third time and a fourth time) to quench my thirst. At this point, it became a challenge to tackle the geyser. Clearly, the water fountain needs repair because it is *IMPOSSIBLE* to get a drink. On the latter attempts, I barely wet my whistle while aspirating most of this "not-so-quenching" refreshment. When I returned back to the office after disappearing for some time, Joe's assistant asked if I would like bottled water. Poetic!

All in all, I missed tub basketball tonight but did read <u>Rhyming Dust Bunnies</u> to Bryce (about five times) followed by a few other books, exercised twenty minutes in my work clothes (I love not dressing for the gym) and now will now enjoy a cup of hot tea, a warm shower and peaceful shut-eye.

What is in a Number?

Today marks day thirty-three of my writing. In my quest for knowledge about the meaning of 33, I learned that this number is significant for healing, compassion, protection and blessing; it is the teacher of teachers, inspiration, honesty and the Angel of Healing and Guidance. As I have always believed, events unfold for a reason and likewise, the signs of life are out there to be read.   How awesome!

Beyond this compelling finding, my high was once again captured in the antics of my loving, energetic and charismatic son. During bath this evening, Bryce, Dennis and I played a game of sink basketball. The goal is simple:

earn 2 points for each successful throw from the tub to the sink. Bryce is rather talented and has quite the arm for a little guy of two years. He scored close to twenty points in the midst of knocking out Kacey, our cat, bonking dad in the head and breaking a few vases. Okay, only the first is actually true. Poor Kacey! She really endures a lot.

Second Day of Chemotherapy

Today was an excellent chemotherapy day. My blood chemistry levels were spot on perfect, and the cancer is really responding to the chemo, even after only one treatment. I could not have asked for better news. My dad and I arrived at 10:00, and I was then whisked off to blood work, a pre-therapy MD appointment and finally, treatment. The whole day from start to finish was 7 hours – home at 5:30.

I attempted to write during treatment except that I had a mild allergic reaction to the first drug infusion. In lieu of Ativan, like the previous time, I was quickly administered a garden variety of steroids, Benadryl and nausea medicine to counteract this reaction. Worked like a charm and once again, I was pleasantly drugged up and therefore dozed off for 1/6th of my time in a rather comfy lazy-boy recliner. My dad on the other hand might have been jealous, as his chair was not so appealing. As a result, there was no likelihood of my writing, which would have resembled more chicken scratch than anything else. I resisted the urge until I could think straight again. At the time, it was physically difficult to talk; my speech and language mirrored more of a drunkard on St. Patty's Day than that of an articulate speech and language pathologist. Chances are I also entertained the nursing staff with my new speech patterns, which was beneficial since I practically closed up the joint. As an aside, everyone at the hospital has been unbelievable – the doctors, nurses and receptionists. Today, Dr. E. gave me a book written by another one of her patients who blogged throughout the process with a similar cancer as mine. Also, the Nurse Practitioner presented a book to me about eating well through recovery. I am truly blessed by these intelligent professionals, family, friends and work colleagues. What an amazing journey!

When I returned home, I had steaming hot dinner waiting from dear friends followed by scrumptious desserts and cookies to devour.

The night proceeded normally with tub time, book time and bedtime conversation with Bryce. He filled me in with all the details of his school day. After chatting and snuggling, we kissed and off to dreamland.

Relaxing Time with Friends

The events of today were characterized by play, play and more play. Bryce's friends, Cam, Olivia and Jack, along with my mom friends, Sarah and Shauna, came to visit. I was able to relax while Bryce had a blast with his buddies – trains, cars and Pirates Tic-Tac-Toe followed by a delicious lunch (compliments of another friend) and sweet dreams at nap time. Not to mention, it was a perfect treat to have loving friends in my company all afternoon. At 3:30, I jetted out to receive my "booster" shot in order to keep my immunities up while Shauna stayed at the house with sleeping Bryce until my husband returned home. The "booster" shot was unremarkable and once again, I feel great. I returned home with an energy boost, exercised on my new Elliptical for a 35-minute date with a famous health doctor on the television, and then devoured baked stuffed shells and asparagus for dinner. For dessert, my favorite – Edible Arrangements, delivered right to my door. I love seeing the truck arrive in my driveway; royal treatment is outstanding. And earlier in the day, we received a Valentine's package. My son is also feeling spoiled by this constant array of surprises. After the first installment this morning, Bryce smiled and asked, "What's next?" Within a few hours, the Edible Arrangement Truck appeared and Bryce exclaimed "YAH!" Hmm, spoiled are we?

After dinner, my friend Bethany came to visit, and we had our monthly "book club" chat. Okay perhaps our meetings could be construed as dorky, but honestly, the quest for knowledge and love of learning is the best way to stimulate a young mind. So the topic for the next couple of months – what else but healthy living!

I am so fortunate to have the consistent kind gestures, conversations and support; the agility of the human spirit is really amazing, and I am blessed. My situation has somehow become a life-changing, upbeat and positive experience, which I attribute to the support of my endearing family, friends and colleagues.

One More Day until Valentine's Day

Today, I tutored a few students in the morning and then went to lunch with my family. During lunch, Bryce yanked at my hair and nearly pulled it off. That would have been quite the spectacle, and certainly, a laugh too! What lies beneath the "hat" is next to nothing – my previously described leopard look is quickly changing to spotty baby spikes here and there. It is so strange. Though Bryce thinks it is the funniest thing, and he frequently requests to see my baldness. As long as he smiles, all is good here. After lunch, Bryce was treated with a "chemo" gift: a new matchbox car that changes color in the water. Mommy was treated with "shut-eye" for a few hours in the afternoon. Pretty standard post-chemo day. For my chemo gift this time, I was thinking hair accessories or some comfy clothes, or, a new piece of jewelry perhaps? Off to bed soon, but anxiously awaiting a McDonald's soft serve ice cream that my devoted husband is fetching for me. Wait, just received a text from him. It reads, "There are 80 elderly biddies buying tea and apple pies one at a time in front of me..." In the midst of unfortunate events, there is always something to laugh about.

Happy Valentines Day

Dennis should write for Hallmark because he wrote me the most sincere card, which made my entire Valentine's Day and by extension, year! While I am thankful for my most amazing husband, I am not so much appreciative of post-Nulasta aches and pains. I physically feel like one of the old biddies from McDonalds, but I am keeping the best energy I can. I even contemplate using the Elliptical for a few minutes.

Putting all that aside, Dennis, Bryce and I ventured to a nearby restaurant and then bookstore for a Valentine's outing. Countless times throughout the day Bryce exclaimed, "I love you mom!" He is the best. It was a nice Valentine's Day.

A Perfect 10

A perfect ten. I am not referring to my upcoming boob job though I am hoping for a good set. But rather, "A Perfect 10" encapsulates the essence of today. My appetite is back – snacking on millet, Brazil nuts and berries. While that may not appeal to the masses, it is my diet of choice these days. And thanks to all the reading about benefits of sleeping and recovery, I intentionally (not really) clocked five daytime hours of sleep. As a result, I feel completely rejuvenated at 10:17 this evening. My biggest dilemma in all of this sleeping is how to handle the bad case of bed head, which evolved. Oh wait, that is not a dilemma at all. On the contrary, my baldness lends to an occasional headache from the constant friction of my scalp on the pillowcase. One day, I will laugh at this experience. Ha, ha!

I Need You Forever

"I need you forever..." the words of my adoring, intelligent and loving little boy, Bryce. Today we were having dinner, and he lightheartedly threw his arms around my neck and exclaimed, "I love you mom. I need you forever." Moments like these are the ones that I cherish and cherish and cherish. Bryce could have asked for just about anything after that display of emotion, and it would have been his. Though already in the last few days, he has magically acquired four new water color-changing cars. A puppet master on a mission – that's my son. Overall, another healthy and strong day seasoned with a sprinkle of shut-eye throughout.

106 and 83

As I sink into the comforts of home, I am mesmerized by the side effects of modern medicine. This evening, I relaxed by the tranquility of a bubble bath, envisioning myself amongst the lush greenery and fragrant flowers of a tropical abode when suddenly I thought it interesting to count exactly how many hairs lost in the single swipe of my follicles. The conclusion – 106 strands released on my left hand and 83 on my right. Quite interesting! While my hair is rapidly diminishing, I have learned that my scalp also needs tender love and care. Therefore, my mom suggested Egyptian Cotton pillowcases. I love it.

Today, the company of friends and family blessed the Phillips household along with two color-changing cars for Bryce, compliments of Nanny. Though, I too was spoiled with a relaxation basket, cheery greetings in the mail and an assortment of bandanas. The night culminated with green tea, a movie and yoga followed by snuggles with my hubby. Smiles, smiles and more smiles...

Children's Games

Today was a relaxing day with my future sister-in-law, Jennifer. We played with Bryce and browsed a few favorite shops. The toyshop was indeed the high of our day, and Bryce finally acquired a favorite game of his after previous references to such over the course of many weeks. This game is the unobtainium of children's games. Though somehow, this particular toyshop had full stock. At first glance, Bryce was elated and would not let the game leave his sight. The rest, as one says, is history. Feeling strong and researching a Disney Vacation Club Membership for another chemo gift.

BRACKA Free

This morning, Bryce, Dennis and I skirted off to a ten-minute appointment at the hospital only to discover that I do not carry the BRACKA gene for breast and ovarian cancer. Great news! The power of positive thinking, meditation, family and friends is in full force.

Apart from morning sleepiness, cured by an afternoon siesta, the day continued with excellence. My friend Liz came for a visit armed with the most scrumptious chicken potpie, creamy ice cream and mouth-watering chocolate chip cookies. A girl's dream! Then, two surprises came via mail – uplifting reading materials as well as a "Baking for Good" package from two other close friends. Thankfully, my siesta was off to a perfect start, sprinkled with inspiration to relax my mind and chocolate brownies to fill my tummy. Though when Dennis realized one of the packages was from "Baking for Good," he beat me to the punch and ate the first brownie. Can you believe it? The nerve of him!

Feeling energized from a three-hour snooze, I prepared dinner, played with my son and anticipated a visit from a dear friend, Megan. The night was sealed with rich and decadent Williams and Sonoma Hot Chocolate topped with whipped cream and marshmallows, endless laughs and amiable conversation.

I Can See the Leaves

A delightful day, yet again! I tutored students in the morning and then enjoyed a delicious lunch with a friend Melissa followed by laughter at the movies with my girlfriend

Bethany. A full belly + lots of laughs = a delightful day.

Healing is a lot like purchasing eyeglasses for the first time. The initial glimpse of the leaves on the trees is breathtaking – the distinction and personality of each leaf is mind-boggling. Three months ago if someone asked me, "Do you feel healthy," I would have in a dumbfounded way replied "sure." In hindsight, this assertion was only partially accurate because now I know what *healthy* can really feel like. Though hard to describe, I am more exuberant, vibrant and relaxed – particularly in this last week. It is amazing and wondrous – the result of an outpouring of positive energy to continually heal.

Laughter continues to be the best medicine. Today Dennis shared a humorous Bryce story with me. In the bathtub, Bryce frolicked amongst the suds and bubbles in typical fashion when unexpectedly a small "log" emerged floating alongside boats and other sea creatures. Ooops! However, there is good news to this story since Bryce finished up on the potty. Later in the evening, Kacey puked on our carpet. Big sigh.

During the revision of this book, it seemed fitting to also include Dennis' version of the "log story." It follows.

The Log Story – Long Form

As much as I love my son, bath time can often drag on, especially when he gets a new toy (in this case, Cars® Color Changers). So today, I used that extra time to shave and buzz my hair. I get in trouble when I make a mess of the sink so I decided to rinse off my scalp and face in the warm bubbly bath. After a refreshing scrub and toweling off, I put my glasses back on to see a healthy log of Bryce poo floating peacefully amongst the shampoo bubbles (we were out of bubble bath, don't act like you haven't done it). "Daddy, I use potty please?" BB asked as I processed washing my entire head with poop water. If this was a CBS 8 pm sitcom, it would be when my wacky neighbor then says, "oh that stinks," and the laugh track would play.

They're regular eggs, just without the yolks (jokes)...Ha, ha!

After my return from an unexpected visit to the hospital, which I will discuss later, Papa Phillips and I engaged in stimulating conversation about Egg Beaters when he explained in his jovial way, "They're regular eggs, just without the yolks (jokes)" ... Ha, ha! A corny aside but still very funny, and we laughed and laughed.

While the conclusion of my afternoon resulted in laughter, the climax was otherwise. After two days of dealing with a painfully sensitive head and a plethora of pimple-like masses scattered along the barren desert, I finally contacted the on-call oncologist who recommended a visit to the emergency room secondary to concerns of cellulitis. Therefore, I packed my pocketbook with my medication list, a mindless novel to pass the time and a refreshing bottle of water. On my way to Worcester, again – my new favorite city! At the emergency room, the nurses quickly whisked me off to the back station, which is away from all the sick folk moping around in the waiting area. I have learned that cancer patients usurp the triage ladder though somehow, I still spent three hours of my day in the emergency room. Regardless of my misfortune in having to go to the doctor in the first place, the visit was actually not so bad. As I patiently waited for a room, I recognized Julie, a nurse whom I met the last time in the hospital. She is truly a delight – kind and thoughtful, a tremendous asset to the emergency nursing staff.

Here, background knowledge is needed. During my last visit to the hospital, Julie and I bonded instantly. She described me as a fighter with a real positive spirit. We chatted some, and she mentioned that her uncle designed "Fight like a Girl; Win like a Woman" sweatshirts to raise money for breast cancer research. This nurse said I seemed the epitome of this mantra. So today when I saw Julie and captured her attention, she joyously ran over to me. With exuberance, Julie explained that her uncle had given her a brown hoodie to get to me the next time our paths might cross. Though Julie wished not to see me under these circumstances, she immediately called her mother who met us with a new styling sweatshirt. I am forever grateful.

All in all, I have folliculitis, which will resolve after a short course of antibiotics. In the interim, I have a textured desert that lines the contour of my scalp. Always an adventure in the Phillips household, but thankfully, no floating poops today.

Sorry Mommy, I No Listen

Today was an ordinary Monday. No striking
news though I did thoroughly enjoy the
company of Aunt Donna. Our day initiated
with "Hello Everybody..." in music class
followed by lunch and nap. Wait, just
kidding. Bryce decided that today, he would
be nap-free. After reading an hour and a half
of books to him (hence the large vocabulary),
I departed the room so he could rest. This
plan did not work, and he was so riled up that
napping was definitively out of the picture.
Concurrent with my ongoing efforts to get
Bryce to sleep, Nancy, who is helping me
keep a tidy house, was downstairs hearing
the ongoing debate between Bryce and me
about the benefits of naptime. Throughout
our dialogue, I realized that rationalizing
with a two and a half year old is not a solid
plan. Ah, we had a rocky afternoon. It

happens to the best of us. All said and done, Bryce apologized – "Sorry mommy; I no listen" followed by an endearing "good night," and all is forgotten. It is great being a mom.

A Blonde Moment

I am reading the signs and figuring my hair will come in blonde. When I arrived at work this morning, I came across a hot pink bag left for me before February vacation. Inside was a warm cozy hat, which will be perfect for the upcoming snowstorm. Though in the search to learn of the identity of my mystery Valentine, I came across a dainty card covered in hearts. Inside read something along the line of "This hat will keep you warm on cold winter nights. Happy Valentine's Day! Love R." R? Who is R? Completely perplexed, I racked my brain for a good portion of the day trying to place a face with "R." To no avail, I finally consulted a friend at work only to realize that "Love" actually said Laura. Oh, Laura R...well that makes sense. I thought I had a secret Valentine. What a laugh!

Wintry Snowy Day

Although a cable wire fell across our driveway this morning, the day continued with less chaos. Initially, ongoing conversations with Comcast were necessary to fix this problem since plow trucks, recycling and trash could not pass. Besides that, I attempted to drive to work, spun out once, and witnessed a horrific accident at the top of my street with an infant in tow! The combination of these events was enough to precipitate the request for a personal day off from work. Therefore, Bryce and I played in the snow, painted, enjoyed a favorite movie, read some books, had lunch and took refreshingly long siestas. Shortly after, Dennis arrived home from work, and we dined in Leominster. Wintry snowy days are the best.

Cycles

On my 48th day of this adventure, I was again blessed with an eternally optimistic spirit, caring friends and divine brownies. Dennis and I thoroughly enjoyed the baked goods, and Bryce relished the toppings – Hershey Kisses, Reese Pieces, etc. So between us three, we "licked all platters clean." At this point, I am a couple of weeks away from chemotherapy, so feeling strong is to be expected. It seems I have a cyclical pattern, which follows.

Day 1 – Chemotherapy.

Day 2 – Still fine, a little tired.

Day 3 – My rockiest day, often extremely tired and a bit achy from my immunity shot.

Days 4-7 – My body continues to recover, and my previous inclination for carbohydrates now shifts to fruits, veggies and millet.

Days 8-21 – With adequate bedtime sleep and regular naps, I am A-okay! Actually, I think I might use this situation as an excuse to nap.

And the cycle continues yet again. This evening, I saw a movie with my friend, Jess. Oh, and very exciting news – Dennis and I bought the second chemotherapy gift today.

A New Hairstyle

As it turns out, it did snow; the meteorologists finally got it right. There is no other career I can think of where one can make mistakes, rather consistently, and still earn a reputable living.

But that aside, today was a good day except for Bryce cranking up the terrible twos, with a vengeance. Listening has been a real issue lately; it seems that a sticker chart and a *good listening recipe* are essential measures to improve his skill in this area. To his credit, he and I ran a lot of monotonous morning errands.

In the midst of our errands, I ran into a grocer who always chats with me at the local market. This morning he perseverated about fifteen minutes on my new hairstyle – asking questions about when I cut it, how I decided on side bangs, the name of my hair stylist and so on. Finally Bryce remarked, "Mama, he wear your wig too?" The guy turned six shades of red. Overtly embarrassed. I clarified Bryce's question and assured the grocer that all was good. Thankfully, it put an end to this uncomfortably long conversation.

At the moment, I am getting ready to enjoy a bubble bath followed by mind-calming yoga. Thankfully, my head no longer sports folliculitis, and the antibiotics are working like a charm. Now that bump-city has resolved, I can actually enjoy baby fuzz on my scalp – very soft! Though being bald does confuse Bryce sometimes, like today, when he called me a "he-she." Soon after, he corrected his mistake. Ah – the things kids say...priceless.

A Mere Day or Two

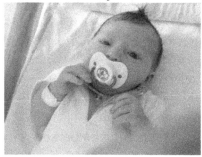

This morning, I was perusing through earlier family photos and came across a favorite. Somehow, Bryce, at a mere day or two, had more hair than I do now. It is quite funny, and he likes to remind me of this fact daily. A typical Saturday afternoon followed. Later on, we had dinner at my parents' home where Bryce enjoyed trains, color-changing cars and silly Uncle Eddy. A quiet relaxing day was just what the doctor ordered.

Almost Halfway

I am halfway through chemotherapy in just four days. In the meantime, I continue to have positive energy and an outgoing spirit. Though today, I took advantage of Dennis being home and slept some because I had a brief headache. It seems that when I slack on drinking (not beer!), headaches and chills develop. As long as I continue to hydrate, the symptoms dissipate. I have also gained a pound or two – damn steroids, or toffee crunch cookies. These baked goods are not positively contributing to a slim waistline. Dennis will have to up the ante a bit and consume some of these delicious goodies. Early night for me since Bryce did not nap, again!

Everyone Poops

With only three days remaining until my third treatment, I am feeling great despite Bryce's recent siesta ban that he saves for mom. For dad on the other hand, he sleeps like a baby. To my good fortune however, Aunt Donna came to visit so a well-needed afternoon rest was accomplished.

In the morning, Bryce and I visited Aunty Sarah, Uncle Dave and their new twin girls. They are absolutely beautiful. Then, Bryce, Aunt Donna and I went to music class when I realized Bryce's inclination to be a teacher's pet. He sits next to Ms. Julie, the music teacher, hugs her, asks about the pitch pipe and requests that she show him how to strum a guitar. Endearing! And during the singing portion of the class, he vicariously belted out the words to "hello everybody." I cannot help but chuckle; he is so cute!

Laughter is the best medicine, and today's amusement came in the way of a book, Everyone Poops by Taro Gomi. Since Bryce does not consistently nap these days, Dennis and I have started story hour/quiet time from three to four o'clock. During story hour today, Aunt Donna was reading about camels, one-hump and two-hump poops, as well as whale poops, when a gentleman arrived at the door to fix our heating system. In the midst of her reading about poop, I was trying to explain to the serviceman about the clunking noise from the furnace when I hear Donna say, "Bryce, do you know what a whale poop looks like?" to which Bryce replied, "yah." Aunt Donna then continued with "I've never seen a book quite like this before Bryce." I nearly peed my pants and had trouble focusing on the current heating situation. 750 dollars later, and with lots of good laughs along the way, we have heat!

The day continued to improve when friends from work brought absolutely delicious home-cooked meals and dessert to my home. What a treat!

Ah, My Knees Hurt

Again, how I laughed today. The hoopla began during an afternoon meeting. A colleague circulated a student-drawn picture of a boy's mom "pole-dancing" with men scattered about frantically waving one-dollar bills. While this illustration was suppose to show the mother's profession, the teacher was naturally curious. Thankfully, the Mrs. provided an explanation The student's mother wrote something along the line of "Honestly, I am not a pole dancer but rather, a worker at the local Home Depot. Recently, I explained to my son that due to the latest winter storm, many shovels were sold. In this picture, I am leaning against a shovel, and the men are simply purchasing ones for the snow storm." Suspect, in my opinion; children are very honest. Hmm??

Later on, I retreated home only to find Bryce in slumber-land while my aunt was relaxing on the couch. Are you kidding me? I could not believe he napped so easily this afternoon. Grrr! Anyway, after catching shut-eye for approximately two hours, Bryce happily awoke with stretches and moans. Out of the blue he grumbled, "Ah, my knees hurt Mama." What??!! I replied.

"Honey, you are two. Why are your knees sore at such a young age?" Bryce continued, "My knees hurt ... like Aunt Donna."   A day earlier when he was on the floor with Aunt Donna, she mentioned, along with poop references, how her knees are sore after sitting on the rug for some time. Bryce does not miss a beat; he is a ham and once again, stirred laughter into my day. After a delicious dinner followed by a game of living room chase, hide n' seek and tub basketball, Bryce finally made it to bed, and mom exercised. A fulfilling day, yet again!

Additional Update:

1. Two more days until my third chemo infusion, and I start my cycle of preparatory drugs tomorrow

Number 34

I will have my third chemotherapy infusion tomorrow. Although no luck is needed; positive energy from all of my loved ones is very much appreciated. Once again, absolutely delicious, healthy, wholesome meals – baked chicken and potatoes, vegetarian chili, baked macaroni and cheese with tomatoes were cooked for us this week.

Dennis, Bryce and I love and look forward to this generosity and thoughtfulness. Furthermore, the variety of literature given to me – both fiction and non-fiction, has been wonderful. While I must bid farewell tonight to get ready for my big day tomorrow, cheers to a positive sign: this evening, I stopped to purchase gas at the nearby Mobil and the pump stopped on $34.34. Both Dennis and I love the number 34; it is one of our favorites. Surely, a good sign!

Third Day of Chemotherapy

Reporting an excellent day at chemotherapy after a HOT night! No, I am not making a sexual innuendo here; on the contrary, I was actually hot. Over the last two nights, I have experienced hot flashes. I can now relate to sweaty women going through menopause. Funny! In the middle of the night, I suddenly felt the urge to splash water on my face, strip off my pajamas (practicing for my next career) and turn the fan to full blast. No covers required. Instead of the sleep number mattress, there should be a sleep temperature mattress; it would have a wide market of buyers, especially women in this HOT stage of their lives.

The morning finally came, and I excitedly sprung from my bed to Bryce's calling "Mama, Dada." Quickly, I dressed him and myself, brushed our teeth and headed downstairs for breakfast. Dennis, Bryce and I were out the door by 7:00 am. On route to Bryce's school, we suddenly realized I did not have my phone or computer charger. This is a travesty. So obviously, being a computer-oriented family, we immediately returned home to retrieve the missing items before venturing off to blood work, a doctor appointment and chemotherapy.

The best news of today was to learn that there is only one remaining palpable mass of approximately five millimeters, which is a huge decrease from the initial three-centimeter diameter. The tumor on the node is barely felt and all other smaller masses have disappeared completely. Dr. E was thrilled by my positive reaction to the therapy, and so early, too. After this appointment, I hugged her and pronounced "Thank you for saving my life" and "I love you!" She gleefully returned with a smile, "I love to be loved." She is a brilliant oncologist. Shortly after, I skirted off to chemotherapy and again, I reacted to the first installation of medicine. Grrr!

Consequently, Dr. E. decided to push more steroids and Benadryl into the IV to equalize my reaction. Worked like a charm and put me to sleep for a good two hours. While I must have needed the rest, I did not accomplish all the tasks I had planned. Tomorrow is another day. In between my bouts of sleeping, Dennis fetched me a delicious salad chock full of vegetables – pea pods, broccoli, red and green peppers, garlic and spinach leaves. I have decided to cut out all refined sugars – no cookies, brownies, sweets in general and rather, stock up on fruits, veggies and whole grains. My vegetable driven salad was a step in the right direction. The day proceeded smoothly, and we finished up around 5:00.

Additional Updates:

1. My bilateral mastectomy will be scheduled earlier than anticipated. After surgery, I will continue Herceptin for eleven more infusions. Fortunately, Herceptin has no detrimental side effects such as fatigue, nausea or hair-loss and is administered rather quickly.

2. Chemo Gift – While I thought extensively about purchasing a heart bracelet from Tiffany's, it may have to wait until the next infusion. Instead, I am going to look for a HEPA air filter, maybe.

Baked Stuffed Sole and Asparagus

Today, Bryce and I enjoyed a morning play date with a friend from music class, Meredith, and her two children Sidney and Ethan. We savored fresh banana bread and shared laughs as the children played amongst the trains and stuffed animals scattered around my house.

In the afternoon, my mom and dad arrived to spend time with Bryce. I rested some and then headed to Worcester for Nulasta. Bryce took a nice long nap for my mom, and she put him down awake without any resistance. What??!! I could not believe it. When he woke up, Bryce and Dennis went to visit Nana and Papa for dinner while I was treated to a baked stuffed sole and asparagus dinner by my mom and dad. Surprisingly, the meal was not so bad, delicious actually, and chock full of OMEGA 3.

Later this evening, I caught up on some well-needed rest and relaxation. Overall, I feel terrific: strong and healthy.

Loss for Words

There are always a few days in the "cycle" when I am at a loss for words. While I physically feel normal, my mind does not work as effectively as I would like. In my writing tonight, I attempted to take a jingle such as "The Twelve Days of Christmas" and manipulate the lyrics, but that did not work. So I decided on a classic entry instead.

In the early afternoon, my friend Brenda stopped by the house. We casually dined at my home enjoying a delicious Keish, fresh fruits and veggies, warm scones and tea. The refreshingly mild weather lent itself for a perfect opportunity to also saunter leisurely through my neighborhood. Later in the afternoon, I retreated to my bedroom for a few hours of rest and then dined with Dennis at a local Grille where I savored sweet potato raviolis. On the way home, we stopped to visit the twin girls, whom I love so much already. They are both precious little angels.

Uh, oh! As I write, I am suddenly experiencing a hot flash. Cool shower required. More tomorrow.

Sleeping Contest

With each cycle of chemotherapy, the aches and pains subside, thankfully. Regardless, ample sleep is necessary to ward off the side effects of chemotherapy. Therefore, I took full advantage of afternoon tranquility in the comforts of my cozy bed.   In competition with Kacey, our cat, I place second, with Bryce trailing in third, for the Phillips sleeping contest. Speaking of which, time to sleep again.

Perfect Spring Day

My little guy's peepers opened wide at 6:30 this morning so our peaceful napping house quickly turned into a "let's get ready and play" jungle gym. Of course, my energy level was consistent with that of a sleepy snail but neither here nor there, preparations for the day began. Between the wee hours of 7:00 and 9:30 this morning, Bryce and I played, ate breakfast, wished Daddy a fulfilling day at work, dressed and awaited Aunt Donna's arrival. At 9:45, Aunt Donna, Bryce and I hopped in the car for music class. As we tapped and bounced to the rhythm of the music, my mild aches and pains subsided a bit and a surge of energy infused me. This new energy compiled with the makings of a perfect spring day and fresh air inspired me to let my hair down and enjoy the cool refreshing breeze. Obviously, this is but a figure of speech these days.

When we arrived home from music, I attempted to warm baked Mac 'n cheese in the oven, but it took so long. Defrosting food prior to cooking is essential. Next time, I will plan in advance. All said and done, the Mac 'n cheese was delicious. While I slept soundly after lunch, Bryce and Aunt Donna played for a couple of hours. At 3:00, Aunt Donna went home (for an afternoon nap, I would imagine), and mom took Bryce upstairs for books and quiet time. Since I felt rested and energetic, Bryce ironically crashed and took a nap. It only figures.

Tattoos and Piercings

After work this afternoon, I ventured off to the mall, scored a sweet tattoo, pierced a few body parts and guzzled a beer. Only kidding, as if I need that disclaimer. In actuality, I ventured home, slept a few hours and awoke to playful laughs and conversation with Bryce. The day was otherwise unremarkable, and I continue to feel healthier with each passing moment.

"Par for the Course" Events of Today:

Hot flashes – in the middle of my afternoon meeting! WHAT??!! Someone please open a window.

Tired Tuesday – It seems the Tuesday after chemotherapy is characterized by a slightly enhanced feeling of fatigue – both mentally and physically. The "deer in the headlights" feeling will pass and tomorrow, 100% Lisa should return. Earlier today, I shared this phenomenon with a fellow colleague, and she mentioned similar observations in herself. She too is undergoing treatment for breast cancer. During a recent class, she reportedly began the day with "Our Father" in lieu of the Pledge. Ah, the laughs, which keep you going!

Sleepy Lisa

Good evening. I am just waking from a long nap on the couch. Evidently, the earlier visit to a few nearby stores wore me out.

Shiatsu

Today's events were peppered with a laugh or two, a Shiatsu massage and an evening visit with a friend.

The Shiatsu body treatment: For those unfamiliar with this practice, Shiatsu is essentially like acupuncture, but without the needles. It was the most infusing, relaxing, exhilarating and mind-calming experience I have ever had, highly recommended. Aaaaah! While the Shiatsu itself was "out of this world" perfect for my mind and body, the ride there was quite the opposite. Of course, the rain plummeted off my windshield, impairing visibility.   But the worst of it was the combination of hot flashes and sauna-like temperatures on route to the salon. Poor Bryce was roasting in the backseat (had to do a midway Bryce swap with Dennis) at the result of mom trying to dry her wig with intense heat. Wet wigs do not make for an attractive hair-do and as luck would have it, it poured during my short walk from work to my car. Unfortunately, I did not have an umbrella.   As a result, my consistently perfect hair day ended up resembling more of a shaggy wet dog.   Anyway, the Bryce exchange was successful; I made it to the massage, and everything turned out just fine. I returned home in the nick of time for Bryce to splash about in the tub, read some books and enjoy stories. After a brief workout and a favorite television program, bedtime calls.

An aside: Today, I received a bill for my recent visit to the ER at the tune of $3132.70. Who knew I was considered an "ER Level 4" patient!? Thank goodness for insurance. My 25-dollar copayment is on route.

Rounds Poem

"Round 1 - Temperature was a wee-bit high, and off to the ER went I.

Round 2 - Folliculitis reared its nasty side, but antibiotics changed the tide.

Round 3 - A UTI thought I, but no, a reaction to chemo - oh my!"

Here I am in the third round of chemotherapy with burning urination. Obviously, a UTI one would think, right? So when my friend Sarah came for a visit this afternoon, I promptly jetted off to Worcester to dispense urine. To my utter surprise, the urine sample was clean with no evidence of infection. In speaking with the docs, I may have a resolving UTI

with traces of symptoms _or_ have a mild
reaction to chemotherapy, which seems more
likely. My oncologist assured me that with
plenty of fluids, cranberry juice and a script
of antibiotics, this new ailment will resolve.
Other than this tidbit, everything else is
status quo. Bryce is a perfect angel, full of
love and energy.

Chemical Phlebitis

The trials and tribulations of chemotherapy
are interesting to say the least. While my
faux UTI is quickly resolving, new
developments always surface. Around five
o'clock, I received a phone call from my
friends at the hospital to relay the good news
that my urine culture was clean. No
antibiotics required. Evidently, the on-call
oncologist did not realize that yesterday, one
of his colleagues already prescribed an
antibiotic for me. After conversing with the
doc, it seems that while there was no urinary
infection, perhaps a smaller virus is the
culprit of my recent ailment. Final plan of
action: finish the script and call with
questions. Questions, I have. In typical Lisa
fashion, I could not let the doctor off the hook
too easily. I took full advantage of his
expertise and inquired as to why the vein in

my left hand was tender a week after chemotherapy.   I learned that I likely have a touch of what is referred to as "chemical phlebitis," which will resolve on its own in due time. For those of my readers, who are not doctors, chemical phlebitis is essentially swelling of the veins due to the IV placement, which is required during chemotherapy.

Later in the evening, my parents came for a visit. Due to the inclement weather, we ordered take out. After dinner, Bryce enjoyed molding animals out of play dough and playing kitchen bowling. Bath, book and bedtime proceeded as usual. With Bryce tucked soundly in bed, my parents and I decided on a romantic comedy as the choice for an evening movie. It was an enjoyable Saturday.

Ignorance is Bliss

All is *a-okay* today. Nothing out of the ordinary and still feeling great! I did however conduct a little research about upcoming procedures. And after viewing some disturbing pictures of lymphedema, I decided it was time to halt the investigation. While knowledge is power, sometimes ignorance is bliss, and better, since not everything you read pertains to your individual situation.

March Showers

I thought the expression was "April showers bring May flowers..." What is up with this rain, rain and more rain? Unbelievable! Despite the weather, I enjoyed smiles and good cheer at music class, relaxed with a book in the afternoon and chuckled at conversations with my son. Always, he says the darnedest things. As of late, Bryce has been quite resistant to my changing his diaper. So I stated frankly in my *teacher* voice, "Bryce, these are your choices. Either mommy has to change your diaper or you need to use the potty." Vibrantly and with stellar eye contact he barked back, "NO, those are YOUR choices!" I should really make a "Top 10 Bryce Quote List." What a card!

Feeling healthy today. No aches and pains, lethargy, nausea, inflammation or urinary tract infections. Still bald, but continue to receive, "I love your new haircut" comments. Funny! Speaking of hair, one of my students nearly yanked it off. That would have surprised him.

Wonderful Day

The rain subsided, finally, and the sun emerged. It was a beautiful day, and I enjoyed basking in the warm sunshine during an afternoon stroll. After school, Bryce and I visited his friend Cam and then returned home for dinner with dad. Later in the evening, I chatted with my friend, Aixa, and will soon relax with a book under my warm, comfy comforter.

Potty on Paddy's Day

I have no new developments regarding my situation. I am healthy and well – eating lots of walnuts, Brazil nuts and almonds, taking my vitamins, lots of fruits and greens and a little dark chocolate. Countdown to chemotherapy begins with only eight days remaining.

What was *most* exciting about today however is that Bryce banned diapers and requested, "big boy underpants like friends, Gregory and Evan." After bath tonight, Dennis went to retrieve a diaper, and BB wanted NO part of it. Flat out refused! Therefore, he is upstairs sleeping in his *big boy* underpants and probably peeing up a storm. Regardless, Dennis and I are elated with this news; we are so proud of him. Bryce asked with a cheeky smile, "that make you very happy?" He is so darn cute. Then, as if the night could not be more perfect, Bryce spontaneously whispered, "you are my best friend" during story time. This brought instant tears of joy to my eyes and once again, "that make you very happy?" He already knows the right strings to pull. Naturally, I snuggled in bed with Bryce for a few additional stories and conversation.

Four Accidents Later

Yes, I did have to clean sheets this morning. But it was worth it because Bryce is a big boy now. All day he wore his big boy underwear and four accidents later, we are still smiling. He is growing up so fast. It is very late right now; I have to sleep. Still feeling great!

It's Official

We are now Disney Vacation Club Members of the Saratoga Springs Resort in sunny Florida. Beyond the excitement of this news, the rest of my day was also wonderful. In the morning, my mother, Bryce and I shopped for an April bridal shower. After browsing several stores and modeling about twenty dresses, an exhausted Lisa returned home without one stitch of clothing. However, there was no shortage of laughs. In the midst of trying on one dress after another, I became extremely skilled at whipping one over my head while simultaneously jumping into the next. During one of these switches, my hair soared over the dressing room door; I nearly peed my pants, I was laughing so hard. Speaking of "pee," Bryce had three accidents today, which is excellent progress from yesterday's data collection of four. Following shopping and laughs, both Bryce and I napped a few hours in the afternoon. At 5:00, I had a lovely visit with friends, Marge, Wendy and Joy. We chatted over Chinese cuisine and played a game called Sequence. Again, there was no shortage of laughs with these ladies either.

The Cake with No Calories

Hold on to your hats; here is to another laugh. In the morning, Bryce and I made sugar cookies. A few days ago, a friend gave me homemade frosting so naturally, it seemed perfect to whip up a batch of cookies to go with this delicious topping. When the cookies were ready, we grabbed the frosting from the fridge and prepared to frost our scrumptious cookies. But to our utter disappointment, Dennis noticed traces of red and assumed it was mold. Bummed out, I sadly tossed the bakeware into the sink and rinsed out the dish. While doing so, I was increasingly disgusted by the volume of mold underneath the top layer of frosting. The mold was so dense that even water did not do the trick to clean the residue. Consequently, I snatched my trusty yellow gloves from the cupboard and manually extracted out the filth, only to discover there was actually a cake below the inch of smooth creamy white frosting. Hence, the cake with no calories! Ha, ha!

Late morning, Dennis' parents came for a visit, and I went shopping yet again to look for something new and stylish for a few upcoming events. My luck turned today, and I was very successful. While Dennis' mom and I were busy shopping, Bryce, Dennis' dad and Dennis washed and vacuumed the cars as well as placed a new light over the driveway. Mid-afternoon, Bryce and I slept. Our good friends, Liz and Andrew arrived for dinner a bit later, and we ordered take-out. Take-out in hand, we spent the rest of the night with our friends and their baby twin girls. Returning much later, Dennis and I put Bryce to bed and then relaxed with a cup of tea and some classic tunes.

Four Days until Treatment Four

Today was a lovely spring day. Bryce and I drove to the farm stand in the morning for hearty fruits and veggies. Afterwards, we visited our friends, Auntie K and Bella for a delicious lunch at their home. We then returned back for a well-needed three-hour nap. Throughout the day, Bryce did well with potty training, only two accidents, which is another improvement. The countdown is on, again, with four days remaining until the fourth chemotherapy treatment. Mom is coming along this time. After this one, there are only two more treatments to go.

Poopy Day: Figuratively and Literally

Today, I encountered two instances of people suffering from diarrhea of the mouth. While they probably had the best intentions, their comments actually felt detrimental to my current situation. I will be honest here. How frustrating it is to hear that my cancer is probably the result of where I live, an environmental factor – "Gee, thanks Jane Doe. Why don't you loan me some money to move then?" How unkind to say such things! Mind boggling, really. Secondly, another person sent me an email from the John Hopkins Institute that provided the fear factors of cancer – i.e. everyone has cancer cells, chemotherapy can cause damage to the system, surgery causes cells to spread, etc. I realize these simple truths, but seeing it in writing was not necessary. While this preliminary information was again, nerve provoking, the subsequent notes about which foods feed cancer were indeed helpful.

On a lighter note, Bryce's potty training took a step backwards with a total of ten accidents – five of each kind. Bryce is a bit under the weather, which may have resulted in poop galore today. At least he did not go in the tub – something positive in light of a messy afternoon. The latter two poops were most hysterical. During the first, he was graciously leaning against the toy box, obviously going.

Naturally I inquired, "Bryce, are you pooping?" He responded with some hesitation as to gather his thoughts, "Um, no I am ... looking at my ... school bus." During the next poop Bryce says, "Mom, I need to go poop." So quickly I ran to him, attempted to carry him to the potty when he remarked, "No, I walk." The walk was more like a nine-month pregnant slow and steady waddle to the potty. Finally, he made it to the bathroom with the end result being, well, you know. Ahhhh! Despite a hectic adventure today, I enjoyed every moment and particularly loved story time this evening.

Big Day Soon

Tomorrow is the big day; thus, I need to sleep. I am so excited, and I always look forward to being one step closer to putting this all behind me.

The support at work is ongoing and amazing. From cards and gift cards to meals and housekeeping, the outpouring keeps going and going and going. At a staff meeting, I expressed my sincere appreciation for everyone and was slightly emotional, which I found strange. I thought chemotherapy was to suppress my hormones and emotional impulses. Guess not! Nevertheless, it was rather funny. After work, I met a friend for a cup of green tea. She too is a survivor and truly remarkable. Soon, we will have a millet and quinoa cooking party to cheer our good health. Later in the evening, I relaxed to prepare for chemotherapy.

Fourth Day of Chemotherapy

Today marks the fourth day of chemotherapy and guess what, the doctors cannot feel the cancer at all in the breast or in the surrounding tissue. The 3-5 mm mass felt during the last treatment dissipated completely alongside palpable masses in the lymph area. So exciting and once again, the medical professionals at the hospital are thrilled, as am I, Dennis and Bryce. My mother came to chemotherapy today; we arrived promptly at 9:00 and followed the typical routine of blood work, appointment and infusion. The infusion began in a room near the nurse's station and patient bathroom but soon after, I was upgraded to a room with a picturesque view of beautiful downtown Worcester. Okay the last part was a bit of an exaggeration, though it was refreshing to have natural light in the room. My treatment began with saline, Pepcid (for my stomach) and Hydrocortisone (to prevent reaction to chemotherapy) followed by the typical concoction of chemo drugs. Due to the miracles of effective steroids, I did not react in the typical chest closing, difficult-to-breath way that I had previously experienced with Taxotere. As a result, Nurse Sharon was able to administer this drug in just over a few hours. I fell asleep at 3:30, awoke at 4:00 and headed home. On route, we quickly stopped for cranberry pills to prevent bladder infection and were greeted by Dennis and Bryce at home.

A quick aside: in my reading, I learned that nipple reconstruction could be developed out of tissue from the labia. Wow!

Nulasta and Hormones

It was a delightful afternoon filled with play-doh, painting, lunch and the movies. Bryce was well behaved, and mom felt strong too. In the afternoon when Dennis arrived home, I left to get my Nulasta shot. The nurses and doctors at the hospital are terrific, so friendly during each visit. Also, I received my hormone levels for both estrogen and progesterone, and based on these percentages, I should respond wonderfully to hormone treatment when chemotherapy and radiation are finished. As for now, I intend to prevent yet another chemical phlebitis from developing on my right hand. Hopefully, dry heat will be the perfect solution.

Smiles and Good Measure

An exhilarating day – a little chilly, but perfect weather to combat incessant hot flashes! This morning, I awoke to the chirping of birds and a light breeze cascading through my open bedroom window. In my opinion, a perfect start to a perfect morning. The day continued with smiles and good measure, as I was able to rest a few hours in the afternoon and then shop with my hubby for Bryce's Easter basket. So much fun! Later in the day, Dennis and I went to a local restaurant for dinner and enjoyed fish and chips complimented with sweet potato fries.

Successful Wedding Shower

Secondary to a mild case of chemo brain, I am having difficulty writing my exact sentiments to describe a perfect day. However, I will give it a go. Dennis and I picked up the blushing bride (my brother's wife to be) a bit before noon to find her blitzed out. Blitzed in the most innocent sense – diamonds, crystals and bling. The chariot continued along to a restaurant in Cranston, Rhode Island where Jennifer was greeted with a cheer by adoring family, friends and colleagues.   The momentum of the afternoon kept me in full swing until about 3:00 when my body decided that rest time was essential. Prior to that, I happily arranged the rehearsal dinner ribbon bouquet while Jennifer's friends assisted with all the other bridesmaid duties. The initial disarray of the ribbon placement reminded me of how mentally disorganized I feel between days three and five after chemotherapy. Nevertheless, I remained in a state of euphoria watching my future sister-in-law rejoice in her lavish presents.   While I was honored to share in her special day, boy was I also thrilled to see my dad. He arrived at the bridal shower around 4:00 and whisked me back home where I crashed soundly into the comforts of my bed for a few hours. Around 6:00, Bryce woke me up with a smile. Immediately, I was flooded with positive energy.   Then he commented, "Mama, you have beautiful eyelashes, but no hair." Ah, back to reality. Ha, Ha! I love Bryce.

Exhausted

I am totally and completely pooped right now so I am going to get some very early shut-eye.

Highlights of the Day:

1. Easter egg coloring with Aunt Donna.

2. Closing on our Disney Vacation Club property.

3. The start of a new music class with Bryce.

4. Interesting looks at the drugstore when purchasing a half-dozen different laxative products for Bryce and me – (side effects of toilet training and chemotherapy).

5. A new water cooler of which the hot spigot does not work.

6. A delicious beef stew, compliments of work friends.

7. Sleepy time with Bryce after stories because Mama could not keep her

eyes open.

8. Delicious green tea.

Still Recovering

When it rains, it pours – literally and figuratively! As the clock struck midnight, Bryce squealed, "Mama! Dada!" Instinctively, we rushed to his bedside to find him covered in vomit. I should have then predicted how the rest of my day might proceed. Nonetheless, Dennis and I diagnosed the situation at hand, worked together effectively to change his bedding and cuddled a sick Bryce into the wee hours of the morning, which came all too quickly. With a still peacefully sleeping Bryce, I took the opportunity to fix myself a bowl of Organic High Fiber Cereal. Big mistake, BIG, HUGE! Something triggered a snowball effect of metabolic changes that resulted in a drenching hot sweat, unsettled dizziness and immediate nausea. Tomorrow, I am sticking with a sugary cereal. Around the same time, Bryce awoke and persisted with questions, "Mama, are you okay?" "Dada, what's wrong with mama?" Other than direct imperatives: "Zofran!" "Motrin!" I could not say anything else for fear of heaving all over the living room carpet. Somehow, I managed to get through this bout with a smile, dressed and went to work. If I were reading this right now, I would be asking, "Why in the world did you go to work Lisa?" to which Lisa would respond, "because I am Lisa, and that is what I do." Well I suppose better late than never, I realized being at work was not the most advantageous option of the day; therefore, I left at noon, returned home and slept another four hours. I then returned to terrific spirits yet again. Phew!

Super Food of 2010: Mangosteen

So in my reading, I learned of a beneficial super fruit called mangosteen. Evidently, non-traditionalists have studied the astronomical and positive effects of xanthones (natural healing substances) on attacking cancer cells. In fact, one particular type of xanthone within the mangosteen fruit was found to outperform five of six commonly used chemotherapy drugs. Impressive? Yes!

So obviously, I sought mangosteen juice at my local farm stand as soon as possible. Having tried it for the first time this evening, I am writing it up as a bit tart, but yummy. Mangosteen will now become an addition to the healthy whole food list alongside millet, swiss chard lettuce and other fruits and veggies. The remainder of the afternoon and evening proceeded with smiles, good measure and Dennis' mom's 60th birthday.

Sleepy Head

It is April Fool's Day. No fooling here. It was a great day. Work proceeded as normal and afterwards, I went for a second Shiatsu treatment. Evidently, it was too relaxing since I crashed with Bryce at his bedtime. My dear friend, Maryann, waited downstairs for probably an hour to watch the beloved Edward and Jacob dual it out for Bella. Poor Maryann sat alone awaiting my descent from upstairs. No such luck.

Signs of Spring

What an absolutely breathtaking day! The weather was perfect for cleaning up the yard, taking out Bryce's sand table and lounging under the warm rays of an uplifting sunshine. During the majority of the morning, Bryce and I enjoyed the outside, at last! "It's bootiful out," Bryce remarked. How is he always so darn cute? Afterwards, we returned inside for a short course of television, lunch and egg coloring. Around this time, Bryce had his one daily accident, which serves as the potty training update. Then, he slept for two and a half hours. Me too! After dinner on the porch, we visited the twin girls, Caitlyn and Nicole. It seems as if Bryce is smitten with Nicole. Hmm?

Mellifluous

Mellifluous. Isn't that a great word? It rolls off the tongue. Earlier today, I was tutoring, and one of my students used this term in our session. Smooth and sweet is its meaning, and a loosely correlated metaphor to describe the perfection of today's weather. Just awesome!

Prepping for Easter tomorrow so I have to write briefly. Bryce was worried that the Easter Bunny would not visit because he did not listen attentively to Mom during book time. However after cuddling and a brief explanation, Bryce went to bed with a smile and reassured that the Bunny will indeed make an appearance.

Easter Day

The day began at 6:30 when Bryce found a trail of Easter eggs from his bedroom door, down the stairs and into the living room. At the end of the trail, an Easter basket chuck full of toys, paraphernalia and other festive goodies were unveiled. In the early morning, Bryce happily played with his new treasures while Dennis and I prepared dinner.

By 9:00 in the morning, we were outside enjoying perfect spring weather with basketball, t-ball and other fun adventures. After several hours, Bryce was wiped and crashed from 1:30 until 3:30. In the interim, my parents, as well as Eddy and Jennifer, arrived for the celebration. Dinner was delicious, and the Easter bunny was good to us all. When Bryce woke up from his nap, he opened more Easter baskets and played the rest of the day. I cannot forget to mention the Easter egg hunt, which was great fun.

Eleven more days remain until my next treatment.

The Wig

The black water cooler arrived, and both hot and cold sides work. Finally. During the installation, it was quite humorous because the serviceman arrived when I sported only a bandana and right before he left, I put on my wig. The expression on his face was priceless as he turned and saw a whole new Lisa. Perfect hair, instantly. I am spoiled by not having to fuss in front of a mirror for hours and then settle on tossing my locks up into a ponytail. Okay, so I never actually fussed for hours – more like minutes, but still. You know, I may continue to wear my wig even after my hair returns. "Blonde Lisa," one day. "Brunette Lisa," the next.

Everything else is going well; I enjoyed absolutely delicious lasagna from a work colleague and was showered with love all day long. I am looking forward to a double date on Saturday with Dennis (obviously) and two other friends – Matt and Janine. Hopefully ADT will not make a visit to our house this time.

Too Many Sweets

Too many sweets; ooops! (Other than that, nothing new to report.) I feel healthy but a little tired, which is probably secondary to a late bedtime last night. Therefore, I am hitting the hay earlier this evening.

A Disjointed Entry

Currently, I am sweltering on my front steps wearing a white tank top and purple bandana. It is quite the sight. My son is on the steps behind me, and my husband is working hard at dethatching our lawn. Ah, my writing must cease momentarily as Bryce just informed, "Mommy, I pooped in my pants and peed in my pants." GREAT! Potty training is not so stellar these days. We'll get there. As quickly as I embraced the warm spring sun, I just as speedily raced back inside for potty time.

I now return, and it is four hours later. After dinner, bath and bedtime routines, I find myself wiped of energy. Need to rest.

Here I am again – two hours later. Secondary to my three and a half hour nap followed by an exhilarating shower, I am completely awake with the time being 12:17 in the morning. Time management is not my strength today. Previously, I was downstairs typing when tapping on the windowpane startled me suddenly. Now, I am upstairs in my bedroom typing away.

Year of No Hair, No Boobs

These entries have come at all different hours over the last few days. My energy wanes so quickly at night whereas in the morning, I am like the energizer bunny. After work this afternoon, I picked Bryce up from school and brought him to a playground. We had a blast driving trucks in the sandbox, whizzing down slides and pretending to be characters from our favorite Disney shows. We also had fun with blocks, dominoes and dinosaurs. On route home, Bryce and I jammed to our new music class CD. The night continued with typical evening routines: dinner, bath, books and bedtime. As of late, Bryce has been interested in coyotes. After he brushes his teeth, we cautiously gaze out the bathroom window to ensure that there are no lingering coyotes in the backyard. Sometimes I will howl and then exclaim, "Bryce, did you hear that?" "Mama, that was you, silly!" he replies. From his bed, Bryce will then warn Dennis to

"Be careful of coyotes" on route to the gym. What a hoot! Apart from playground smiles and coyote stake-outs, I learned that post mastectomy, my insurance will cover two sexy bras, two camisoles, one full and one half prosthesis. This year will be the year of no hair, and next year will be the year of no boobs.

Do You Want the Can, Sir?

Today began with a dry pull-up, but ended with two poopy big boy underwear. Bryce valiantly tries to remember and 60% of the time, he does a wonderful job. The other 40% is a combination of making it to the potty, going on route to the potty or avoiding the potty completely. It is a crapshoot – literally and figuratively.   Earlier in the day, Bryce and I went to visit the twins, again. Later on, we adhered to traditional afternoon routines of lunch, playtime and nap. At some point in this mix, I spotted Bryce feverishly pushing against the toy box – very statuesque. "Bryce, what are you doing?" I asked. "Uh, looking at my car" was his reply. "Bryce, are you pooping? Should we go potty?" Bryce stood up refreshed and said, "No, I already went Mama." Not wanting him to hold it in, I praised him up and down for pooping his pants.

In the evening, I visited a friend, Bethany, to watch a very funny movie. During one part in this movie, the main character was on a flight when the attendant asked him, "Do you want the can, sir?" I laughed, especially since the character was completely taken aback trying to process exactly what the attendant was asking of him. This is a classic example of the supra-segmental quality of language.

The drive back home was peaceful, and my loving husband and sleeping son greeted me.

Updates:

1. We are official Disney Vacation Club owners.

2. Six days until my fifth chemotherapy treatment.

Blown Away

What a memorable day!

In the morning, I tutored. During the afternoon, I rested some and played with Bryce. Today, sheet tents were the activity of choice. Bryce pretended to be a ghost, and boy was he terrifying. Nancy, my best friend,

also came for a visit. She and I watched a
movie during Bryce's nap. And fortunately,
Nancy stayed into the evening so Dennis and
I could spend time with friends, Matt and
Janine. Once again, we dined at our favorite
steak house in New Hampshire. There is
something about this place because each time
we go there, a wild and unimaginable story
unfolds (remember ADT). Dinner proceeded
normally, apart <u>slow</u> service, and I do mean
slow. We arrived at 7:30 and did not finish
up until about 10:30. Later on in this drawn-
out-dining-experience, the waiter
persistently attempted to use his crumber
(yes, this is the actual name) to remove
crumbs from our table. After at least six
attempts to get a cherry stem onto the
crumber, I finally picked it off the table and
placed it on his fancy tool. The whole scene
was extremely comedic and as a result,
Jannine and I were in a laughing fit with such
exuberance that it brought tears to our eyes.
Dennis and Matt just stared. However, it was
not until we left the restaurant that the night
really began. At the doors leading to the
parking lot, Matt's friend, Joe called from
across the way. Matt loves to ride
motorcycles, as do his buddies. Having such
an enjoyable evening and feeling in

great spirits, Joe jokingly asked me if I were interested in riding on the back of his bike. I am not sure what I was thinking when I said "yes" – a reckless move to say the least. Nonetheless, I thought it would add to my evening of spontaneity and fun. Against Dennis' better judgment, I went. At first, I enjoyed the ride until the wind blowing through my hair began to strengthen with the acceleration of his bike. While he was a safe driver and did not exceed speed limits, evidently, the wind was too much for my hair. Unexpectedly, my wig sailed off in a gust of wind. Oh my! Fervently, I was bellowing to Joe to stop the motorcycle to find my wig, which was now somewhere on the side of the highway in New Hampshire. I am having difficulty describing the extent of the panic, laughter and magnitude of the situation. After tonight, I am officially adding, "Do not ride motorcycles" to the list of cardinal rules for wig care. Dennis found my leaf-ridden wig, after about forty minutes of searching, in a bush about a half-mile from the restaurant. While very stylish, the lime green bandana is not as becoming as my totally perfect hair, minus the leaves. I am thankful for Dennis' keen eyesight. Without question, this night topped the ADT fiasco.

P.S. **Blown Away** is a late April Fool's entry. Ha, ha! No motorcycle adventures, honestly. That night, I did go out with friends, but the "wig sailing off in a gust of wind" was simply, a hoax.

Inspiration

I slept in today, until about 8:30. Earlier than that, I am typically in rough shape. I am not a morning person, even being a mom. Shortly after, Nancy woke up; we had breakfast together and played with Bryce. Also this morning, Bryce took a pretend boat ride with Aunty Nancy while on a mission to save our cat.

In the afternoon, Bryce and I enjoyed beautiful weather, weeded my gardens and drew a chalk road, which covered most of the driveway and front steps. Around 1:00, we dined in the kitchen. Bryce loves rice. Who knew? "Mama, I want more please." Other than that, the day marched on in sync with typical expectations and no new updates. Actually, I did have a dream last night that doctors ran all my repeat scans and found me cancer free. That was awesome.

Many have called me an "inspiration;" however, it is really those people that inspire me daily with ongoing sentiments, meals, gift cards, smiles, laughs, friendship and love. So I thank *them* for being *my* inspiration too.

Yum – Crackles

For the fifth time, the countdown is on until my next chemotherapy session. Dennis will be coming with me this time, and our hope is to narrow down upcoming dates for surgery and radiation. The current thought is end of May or beginning June for surgery secondary to my positive response to treatment.

Other than that, today was a lovely day sweetened by family visits and the most delicious sugary chocolate cookies called crackles.

Two More Days

Two more days! I am looking forward to treatment five and then, putting it behind me. Almost there! In the interim, I am diligently thinking of my laundry list of questions.

Today was busy at work – flooded with meetings, therapy sessions and consults. But in the midst of a hectic morning, a colleague surprised me with hand lotion – a necessity during treatment for breast cancer. After work, I wrapped up the day with some tutoring and then went to Concord, Massachusetts to visit with my friend, who birthed an adorable little lady, Olivia.

I arrived back home in the nick of time for dinner and playtime with Bryce. Speaking of the darling Bryce, I am happy to report having a day void of any accidents. Without doubt, this beats the recent ten accidents from just a short time ago. Furthermore, Bryce's teacher, Cam, stated that Bryce is a thoughtful friend to the other children at school. What a high for Dennis and me!

After nightly routines, I had an enjoyable conversation with a new friend, Colleen, and then exercised. Spurring from my chat with Colleen, who is an oncology nurse, I learned that shells or items from the ocean are said to have healing powers. She explained that some of her patients have necklaces with shells to facilitate serenity and peace. A terrific idea!

Twenty Loads Later

One day left until chemotherapy, and there is

never a dull moment. After work today, I picked Bryce up from school to run a few errands and return home to see Dennis. When I arrived at school, Bryce's teacher, Cam, explained that another student had head lice. So immediately, I called our doctors. Each of them highly recommended that I wash sheets and stuffed animals as well as any plastic toys that Bryce may have played with in the last few days. Well that is just about everything. Therefore, my relaxing evening ended up being full of laundry, laundry and more laundry. I ran four loads at my house and sixteen more at the laundromat. By the end of the night, our entire house was spic and span.

Finally getting to the mail, I received a thoughtful bracelet from my cousin in North Carolina that read, "Onward...Upward," my mantra through all of this.

Fifth Day of Chemotherapy

Tax day has an entirely new meaning for me in light of current events. Dennis and I sit in this cubicle of toxins, as I receive Benadryl, steroids (two dosages were need this time), a saline flush, Taxotere, Carboplatin and Herceptin followed by an hour of fluid. Whew! That was a mouthful.

Despite the massive amounts of drugs pumped into my body, I am thrilled to report positive outcomes. Dr. E., whom I love, stated my breast exam is now considered normal with no evidence of cancer. At surgery, she predicts Dr. Q will find I had a complete pathological response to chemotherapy. Dr. E. was so confident that in jest, she declared to relinquish her son to me if she were wrong. No adolescent for me; thank you very much. Bryce will be there all too soon.

On another note, my meatless days left me with a touch of anemia while the potent drugs irritate the lining of my bladder; luckily, remedies are simple and include a steak weekly and cranberry tablets daily.

Below is a list of upcoming events:

1. Meeting with my surgical oncologist in early May to schedule surgery for the first week in June.

2. My next and last chemotherapy session is May 6th.

3. A Breast MRI and CT Scans are scheduled for mid-May. The bone scan will be later this same month.

4. Radiation will begin end of June and continue through the middle of August.

5. My reconstruction will be sometime in February, six months post radiation.

Mammography

I just returned from my Nulasta injection, and a few modifications were made to my upcoming May schedule, which will also include mammography. Great! My boobs will be squished yet again. All other events remain the same, as of today, anyway. Flexibility is key in this process since appointments change and move around at a moment's notice.

Chemotherapy and Childbearing

Dealing with the aftermath of chemotherapy loosely parallels childbearing. Having a baby is grueling and exhausting, but then you forget because you have the most amazing love in your arms. In my case, my dear Bryce who gives me strength with his kindness, thoughtful gestures and words – i.e. "Mama, I need you forever" (not to mention bedtime cuddles). While today was downright tough, I know I am more a beacon of health with each passing day. And in a few short days, I will somehow forget today's arduous journey in the aftermath of chemotherapy. That being said, I am off for shut-eye now. In the morning, Bryce and I are making green eggs and smiley pancakes.

The Aunts

Birds are chirping; spring is in the air. These are all positive signs of things to come. This morning, Bryce and I made our way out of a sleepy slumber to enjoy smiley fruit pancakes and loads of playing. In the morning, a phone technician installed a fiber-optic network in our house. Bryce and I jarred Dennis from a sound sleep to meet the guy. Later on, Aunt Cookie and Aunt Donna visited Bryce. I like to think they were coming to see me, but no, that is not really the case. I get it, I do; after all, Bryce *is* the cutest. Anyway, they really laid on the silly for him and all together, we enjoyed couscous for lunch and cupcakes for dessert. Since I was not feeling my best, I rested a few hours. Right before nodding off, I heard Aunt Donna exclaim, "I love Everyone Poops." Even though I knew she was referring to a book, it struck my funny bone nonetheless.

One Hundred Days of Health

Today marks the 100th entry since the initiation of my writing. For celebration, Dennis and Bryce made me a sweet spice cake with butter cream frosting. Yum! But even with a sugar high, I rested quite a bit throughout this climatic day. Our friends, David and Sarah, also came for cake. And after all the excitement, I now feel eager to turn in for the night. Though before I do, exciting news: Bryce debuted a poop in the toilet all on his own. He was so proud. Us, too!

Five Bryce Laughs

I am approaching normalcy, once again, after a seemingly long recovery from chemotherapy this time. Thankfully, it is onward and upward from here. My aunt came for a visit today, and we shopped about here and there. Bryce kept us entertained beginning with "Harold" at the local bookstore. We were making our way toward the train table when Bryce spontaneously pronounced, "Yah, Harold is here." My mind races ... *Harold, Harold, who the heck is Harold* when I then realize Bryce is vigorously pointing to a display of "Harold" from a famous children's book. *Laugh number one.*

Our journey continued with an early nap to break up the day. Post-nap, Bryce and I walked to the baseball field near our house to get an ice cream. On route, we were chatting about different things when he commented, "Mama, I think I need some Chapstick. Did I use the right word?" *Laugh number two.* Background: As of late, Bryce is working on differentiating *lipstick* from *chapstick.* Dennis and I explained that girls wear lipstick, but anyone can wear chapstick. This is an ongoing conversation.

On the way back home, our conversation continued. We saw a UPS truck drive past. Bryce: "Mama, hurry. It's UPS. Maybe they bring me a bike, or a scooter, or a new mailbox to my house? Hmm, what will it be?" *Laugh number three.* Evidently, we need a bike, scooter and new mailbox.

Fast-forward to bedtime. Mama was summoned to find Bryce. "Hmm, is he in the bookshelf?" "Hmm, is he under the bed?" "Hmm, is he in the windowsill?" and so on. Following a game of *Mom finds Bryce*, Bryce decided that it was his turn. "Hmm, is she in the bookshelf?" "Hmm, is she under the bed?" "Hmm, is she in the windowsill?" *Laugh number four.*

The night ended with bedtime stories defined by Bryce's imagination. Today's version follows.

> *Mickey was meandering through the depths of the dark forest when suddenly he heard a crunch. "What could that be?" Mickey exclaimed. Then, he realized he stepped on Donald. Oh no! What will he do?*

Bryce's solution: "Go to the doctor and pump him up." After Mickey pumped up Donald, they went to the playground and lived happily ever after, or so Bryce tells me. *Laugh number five.*

Other news:

1. I could flood the Nile with my hot flashes.

2. Bryce tells me he is "thankful" for all the people that help mommy. So cute. So true.

Little Golfer

A delightful and sporty day! In the morning, Bryce and I played the role of enthusiastic baseball fans at the practice down the road. "Go team!" he exclaimed. "Mom, he missed it!" We then had lunch and drove to Lancaster Golf for driving range practice. Bryce grabbed his pitching wedge, and off we went. I was actually impressed by his golfing. We had a blast. After driving a small bucket of balls, we inhaled orange sherbet with gummies and next, stopped at a clothing store for a great sale. Nap, dinner and evening routines followed accordingly with a movie to close out the day.

Trip to the Ocean State

Six-thirty came all too quickly as Bryce beckoned, "Mommy!! Daddy!!!" I would love to report that I excitedly hopped out of bed, ready to start the day. Not so much the case but still, I cherished cuddling with my love bug. Around 7:00, I finally descended to the kitchen, ready for my Mangosteen fruit smoothie and sweet rolls. Around the same time, a case of Mangosteen juice was delivered. This energy-infusing drink hit the spot for the eventful day ahead. The first stop was a bridal shop in Rhode Island to pick up my princess dress for Eddy and Jen's wedding. After a few minor alterations, particularly the waist and chest area, I should be able to "bust" a move (insert laugh!) By

10:30 this morning, Bryce and I made it through the flood zone of Warwick, Rhode Island for lunch with Auntie Jen. After lunch, Bryce was fitted for his tuxedo, and invites were picked up for the wedding. Eventually, we made it to the beach. "I am having so much fun," says Bryce, soaked to his knees from splashing in the ocean. A spectacular day!

The Next Morning

I awoke to the melodious sound of birds chirping in the wee hours of the morning. Freezing, I tiptoed to the window in all hopes that I would not wake Bryce from innocent dreams. Of course my internal temperature changes with the moment, so feeling completely hot last night I opened all windows in the guest bedroom at my brother's house; I certainly paid for it this morning.

By 7:00, Bryce was ready to start his day so naturally, he woke everyone else up too. Once awake, or semi-awake, we gobbled up tasty Belgium waffles and watched a children's movie. Shortly after, Bryce and I dressed for the zoo and met Nanny and Granpa, our friends Mike, Nancy and Marie, as well as Marie's two boys, Shane and Luke.

Family Day

"Up and Adam!" An early start to the morning beginning at Nana and Papa's house for breakfast – bacon, sausage, eggs, Mickey Mouse pancakes, fruit and juice. Yum! Aunt Cookie is heading back to California, and we will miss her.

Laugh Number One. Dennis' mom put her cell phone in a washing machine cycle. Nana! The solution: MacGyver Phillips (this is what we call Dennis' dad because he has an uncanny ability to fix anything by the simplest of methods) retrieved the drenched cell and placed it in a bag of rice. Lo and behold, the plan worked; the rice absorbed the moisture from the phone, and Nana is chatting away once again.

Laugh Number Two. Bryce asked me, in the midst of a scorching hot flash, "Mama, are you hot from the sun or from the light?" I wish it were that simple. Ha!

After a few chuckles at Nana and Papa's house, Dennis, Bryce and I drove to Rhode Island for Sunday dinner with Nanny, Granpa, Auntie Jen and Uncle Eddy. The menu featured delicious spinach leaf salad, ham, potatoes, an assortment of veggies, strawberry shortcake and ice cream cookie sandwiches for dessert.

On route home, Bryce, Dennis and I were chatting when Bryce exclaimed, "I know what you can get me for my birthday ..." and he continued with a list of three items: a bucket, rolling pin and stroller. This list coincides perfectly with the "UPS Wish List" of a bike, scooter and mailbox. Ah, Bryce!

A week and a half remains until my final treatment. How the time has flown! Also, I am not sure if this is a side effect of anything, but today, my feet were unusually stinky. Hey, if you cannot laugh at your own expense, who can you laugh at?

Choices

On a good streak, as normal in this part of the cycle, with only a few days left until my next and <u>final</u> treatment. Again, I cannot believe it. Today was a lovely day with music class, lunch, siesta and tutoring later on.   Sprinkled generously throughout were Bryce's smiles, laughs, energy and humor. For example, Bryce gave Dennis "choices" before bed. My little parrot said, "Dada, these are my choices..." and he continued with potential options.

In the evening, I shaved for the first time since January. Shave! Now one might be thinking, "What? That is disgusting." But strangely, I did not need to until now. Trace amounts of hair grew over the previous week. Even on my head, the fuzz stretches upward about a half inch. This is very exciting considering the recent drought of this commodity. Like Edward says to his sister Elizabeth, in <u>I Wish I Was Sick, Too!</u> by F. Brandenberg, "The best part of being sick is getting well..." My thoughts exactly!

Mild Anxiety

For the first time really, I felt mild anxiety about the upcoming mastectomy. I know it will go over well because my surgeon is amazing. Patients have called him the "miracle maker." But still, I have several questions, as normal. The surgery will be here before I know it. Then, I can put this, too, behind me.

On an unrelated note, Bryce bought me a lovely heart necklace. He is the best.

Bone Scans

Today was normal; I feel healthy through and

through. After work, Dennis, Bryce and I went to a restaurant for dinner preceded by ice cream for dessert. Yes I write, "preceded" because we had ice cream first. All is good; we ate our dinner too.

Tomorrow, I have a bone scan. Again, I am aiming for "beautiful bones."

Two Hundred and Something

With radioactive dye coursing through my body prior to the bone scan, I felt a surge of energy and contemplated walking to a nearby bookstore from the hospital – a distance of two miles between locations. But after consulting my iPhone map, I realized this excursion would take over an hour round trip, which would not leave enough time for lunch and relaxation. Instead, I hopped in my Honda CRV and drove through a windstorm (really, it was) to the bookstore.

After lunch, I returned back to the hospital for the bone imaging. I was approaching the entrance of the building when two guys whistled at me. Funny! I continued to the door and subtly shifted my hair around. The guys exchanged a brief, but confused look with each other, and I chuckled under my breath.

During the bone scan, two hundred and something is the number I reached before falling asleep under the bone scanner. But yet again, I have "beautiful bones" and an additional "straight spine."

All said and done, I returned home. Dennis was mowing the lawn, and Bryce was running around. Shortly after, we ate dinner. Then, I squeezed in a quick workout before my friend, Maryann, arrived for a movie. Round two. No sleeping this time, like the last, when Maryann was left to her own devices in my living room while I slept peacefully upstairs with Bryce. Despite my neglect (insert smile), Maryann still wants to join me in chemotherapy next time. What a good friend!

The rest of the night included hot flashes, one after another.

Fun Friday

I have had a string of positive days over the last week, and Bryce and I enjoyed a perfect spring day today, yet again. The morning began leisurely with banana pancakes and egg white veggie omelets for breakfast followed by a game of hide n' seek octopus tag. An hour later, we got dressed and spent the following hour on the deck chatting, eating goldfish crackers and cleaning up the sand table. Before lunch, Bryce had a rather large number two accident. In the midst of my changing him, a small amount of poop smeared onto my hand. Gross, but par for the course! Anyway Bryce noticed this and says, "Mom, you have poop on your hand. That's disgusting!" Thank you Captain Obvious. His commentary keeps me on my toes at all times. Midday, we settled down for a relaxing lunch. The rest of the day's events included a trip to the hardware store, forsythia planting and quiet time (in mom's world – nap time!) We both woke up later to then enjoy a healthy snack and quick drive to dad's softball game, where Bryce and I were yet again, two adoring fans. Go dad!" Bryce exclaimed. Bryce loved watching him play, and I loved being with my two guys. Even though this game was a highlight of my day, the very best moment was captured in the sentiment of my loving son when he spontaneously shared, "Mama, you're my best friend." You too, Beebs! You too!

Poolside Surgery

I had the most bizarre dream last night. Dr. Q. decided to operate poolside so the ambience would soothe my anxieties. All went well, and I came out of surgery with a smile and a new look. Having such an interesting dream, this morning, I awoke and immediately titled this entry so I would not forget. However the best part of it is that soon, this dream will become a reality. While I will not be sipping martinis in a pink bikini while the doc is lopping off my boobs, I will be able to put this ailment behind me in exactly one month from today. Huge smile and relief, too!

Three Years Young

United Parcel Service arrived, again, to deliver Bryce's third birthday party supplies: plates, napkins, favors and entertainment. I cannot believe he will be three so soon. What a year!

Endless Thoughts

Two more days until chemotherapy, and this treatment is the last one of six. In the morning, I was reflecting with a friend about this journey. Both in awe and with watery eyes, we shared a smile in knowing how far I have come since the beginning. Like it was just yesterday, I recall the afternoon my mom and dad came over and masked their disbelief with sunglasses – trying so hard to be strong. We had the best day; we played with Bryce and just enjoyed each other's company, which was difficult considering the circumstances. I also remember, so vividly, the day when my mother-in-law Debbie, Dennis and I went out to lunch after finding out the details of my cancer. We toasted to a successful journey ahead. I will always remember the hug from my father-in-law, which embraced me with the message – *it is going to be okay.* The sincerity in everyone's gestures have since continued and strengthened from these initial graces of love and support. Beneath it all, Dennis has been my rock, the unsung hero and the one I do not thank enough. He is always there for me, for Bryce and for our family. He is the one who keeps me strong when I feel worried or stressed; he is the one that keeps everything going when I am dealing with chemotherapy side-effects, and he is always supportive through thick and thin. For this, I thank him.

Sappiness aside, two laughs follow:

1. On reconstruction – No nipples required.
   Therefore, I will not have to worry about
   the imprints of them through my shirts
   during cold weather.

2. On hot flashes – When putting Bryce to
   bed, he furiously fanned himself with his
   blanket and told my husband, "I have hot
   flashes Dada." Oh no! He could be in the
   Guinness Book of World Records.
   Headline reads: "First 3-Year-Old with
   Hot Flashes!"

The Staircase Journey

Work, an ophthalmology appointment and
quick stop at the local pharmacy began the
day. Later on, I met a friend Melissa for
dinner. Melissa is also a speech and language
pathologist and in our conversation, she
shared a few details from a session that she
had in the morning. The student Melissa had
worked with was having difficulty in her
French class. Melissa explained to the
student that learning new information is like
traveling over a staircase. On the way up, the
journey can be arduous and undesirable, but
you are learning. When you finally reach the
top and then descend, your experience

is relaxing and fulfilling, especially as you reach your goal on the other side. I am excited to be on this descent now. Health. Yah!

Sixth Day of Chemotherapy

Today was certainly a milestone in its own right. It was my sixth and <u>final</u> day of chemotherapy. Strangely enough, I will not have to schedule another appointment in three weeks. Rather, my next appointment with Dr. E is in the middle of June. At that time, I will receive my infusion of Herceptin as well as discuss future plans to facilitate long-term health. In the meantime, I have a laundry list of appointments next week and prior to that, I have a Nulasta shot tomorrow afternoon. This shot has also been called the "New Nasty" secondary to the crappy effects it leaves you with shortly after the injection. I relate. Nevertheless, it will keep me healthy.

Appointment Updates:

1. There are zero palpable lumps to be felt, and my doctor is thrilled with progress to date. She states that *if* there were rogue cells in my body, they are likely to be gone as well.

2. After my appointment with Dr. E., I proceeded to my usual window spot for therapy. Lucky for me, I had an elderly, questionably insane American Idol Contestant, and not a good one, belting out at top of her lungs, "Happy International Gay Nurses Day!" over and over. Quite a lady, but her behavior spurred a chuckle. Since I drink five gallons of water each day (an obvious exaggeration), I always need a bathroom. Therefore, I thought it best to go prior to Taxotere, which I always have a reaction. So during my Benadryl infusion, I went to the ladies room. Evidently, this was not a good idea either since I could not recall which corral Maryann and I were in. Thankfully, she saved the day and summoned me to the right spot. The dreaded Taxotere was next after these pre-medications. Of course, I would

end this treatment with a bang and naturally, I reacted as "planned." Hydrocortisone dulled the effects, and I fell asleep for two hours. When I arose, Maryann and I chatted some, scheduled upcoming appointments and called it a day.

Additional Updates:

1. My chemotherapy/Mother's Day/ anniversary gift is a Movado watch. It is beautiful: two toned – silver and gold with diamonds, too. It will always remind me that time is of the essence.

2. Even more special was the plant Bryce grew and gave me for Mother's Day. What a sweet little guy!

Reader's Digest Version

Here is the reader's digest version of today secondary to my increasing level of fatigue this evening. I am essentially sleeping while I write this entry. Drool is dripping. Just kidding.

1. Played with moon sand during breakfast on the deck with Bryce.

2. Ran a few errands culminating at a local farmland, which Bryce loves.

3. Nap time with the Bryce.

4. Nulasta Shot.

5. Girls night.

6. Bedtime.

Tomorrow may be more interesting.
Random aside of today – everything (except
pasta and sauce) tastes like metal. Weird!

Holding Steady

Today I felt emotional when thinking about
my final stretch in recovery. Beyond the
metallic taste in my mouth, all is good. This
morning, my future sister-in-law and I had a
delicious breakfast to start the day off right.
We each continued our way with my day
involving lots of sleep and Jen's with wedding
planning. Last night was the best girl's night
– laughs, laughs and more laughs. As for
tonight, I am turning in early. This week, I
have several appointments coming up.

Happy Mother's Day

Today is the last of the dreaded Sundays post
chemotherapy and more importantly, it is
Mother's Day. Right now, I am having major

writing block. I also continue to taste metal, which does not help. Not that I have consumed metal before, but perhaps this taste is what it would be like. Yuck! This entry is an exemplar of true stream of conscience. I love my husband and son. Despite my lethargy and aches (and did I mention the metallic taste in my mouth?), it was a perfect day. Next week, Bryce, Dennis and I will celebrate Mother's Day at a baseball game. I cannot wait. Hot flash coming on! Good night.

ZZZ...

Although today is the last of the sleepy Mondays, it was indeed sleepy. Consequently, I dozed off with the Bryce at bedtime. And once again, I am going to bed.

Chemo Brain Tuesdays

While I attempted the entire afternoon to ward off the effects of chemo brain, it did not work. I could not process language, which is definitely a problem in my position as a speech and language pathologist. Nevertheless I made it through, and here I am.

After work, I met my boys for a Mother's Day dinner consisting of salad, mushroom risotto and baked macaroni and cheese. Scrumptious.

Additional Updates:

1. Bone scan was 100% clean.

2. MRI is tomorrow.

3. Mammogram (Damn! I have to squish my boobs in the "boob squisher" again) and breast ultrasound are Thursday.

MRI

The day began with Jimmy Buffet and the clanking of an MRI machine. While jamming to the tunes of JB is better than my previous experience listening to advertisements for a local state college, the decibel level of this technology is far too high for the human ear to safely process. At the end of twenty-seven long minutes, the headrest imprinted a mark on my head while mild throbbing continued for a few minutes longer.

Afterwards, I went to work for a half-day and then hit the farm stand. While there, I came across mangosteen fruit. The mangosteen was mouth-watering. I bought a whole bag and already devoured most. Continued positive energy transfused during my Reiki treatment. The clinician stated that I have a "highly intelligent body." What does that mean? If nothing else, it was relaxing.

Your Nipples Could Turn Black

In my travels today I heard someone say, "positive thinking leads to a happier, healthier life." How true! Today, I met with Dr. Q, my surgical oncologist, to review the upcoming mastectomy, which is scheduled for June 1st. In our meeting, he reviewed my record, discussed the pathology of my cancer. Wait stop a minute. Cancer? What cancer? Guess what?! There is no cancer. All, and I do mean all of my imaging was clean. The previously seen *clouds* of cancer underlying the calcifications are gone, and the breast MRI was totally free of any indication that there could be cancer, even in the lymph node. What a relief! I dreamed of this day. So yes, "positive thinking leads to a happier, healthier life."

Dennis and I continued conversation with Dr. Q. when he abruptly stopped and questioned,

"Oh, do you want to save your left nipple?"
Well that is something I never thought I
would hear. My answer: "no thanks."
Especially, no thanks, after I learned that if
blood flow did not return with enough
immediacy to the chest wall, the nipple
would turn black and need to be removed
anyhow.

It has been an exhilarating day; one I will
always remember. However, I must go to
sleep. I have chest and abdomen CT scans
tomorrow.

Chest and Abdomen CT Scan

"Breath in ... hold your breath ... 3 - 2 - 1
release ..." After six or so repetitions of a
robotic man's voice dictating my every
respiratory move, the days of scans were just
about through. However, this particular scan
seemed to continue on and on. Interestingly,
the dye that was injected warmed my entire
self and also stimulated the feeling of having
to pee. Quite a way to start the morning! Oh,
but there are positives in light of every event.
I was treated with twenty ounces of a
delicious barium sulfate smoothie prior to
the CT. After the scan was complete, I
returned to the dressing room to catch a

glimpse of an older man in his tighty-whities and coordinating tank top. Yuck! These gowns have ties.

New Appointments:

1. Dr. C, my radiation oncologist is meeting with me Monday.

2. I will be fitted for a compression sleeve and gauntlet to prevent post-surgical swelling on Tuesday.

Let's Go Paw Sox

Dennis and I took Bryce to his very first baseball game in my home state of Rhode Island. Between enjoying traditional ballgame snacks and the many purchased souvenirs, cheering was a blast. "Let's go team," Bryce chanted alongside the other of adoring fans. We made it until the eighth inning and then headed back to the comforts of home. It was the best time. Our seats were so close to the field. I love my boys, and what an exciting Saturday night we had! "I had so much fun," Bryce exclaimed as we left.

Cancer News:

1. Or, should I say lack thereof! I am still on cloud nine. What a victory, but I thank my lucky stars.

2. I feel almost back to normal barring occasional nosebleeds – grrr!

Preparations

Exhausted right now. Phew! Dennis and I prepared our house for Bryce's huge upcoming third birthday bash. Preparations included mulching the beds, planting perennials and annuals as well as weeding through Bryce's toys. As soon as Bryce was in bed, Dennis and I also crashed. Tomorrow, I have an appointment with my radiation oncologist. For now, shower and meditation are needed.

Four Updates

The reader's digest version, again, of my updates follow.

1. A few of my fingernails are bruised and partially coming off; I neglected to use tea tree oil after my last treatment. Big mistake. Fortunately, the local market had it in stock so I am in better shape.

2. Mid morning, I met with Dr. C who is the oncologist that will decide on my radiation treatment. I have another appointment to plan the specifics and mark the radiation field with tattoos. But for now, an initial examination and consultation were provided. During the examination, Dr. C. had a medical student shadowing her every move. This gentleman attempted to conduct a breast exam though it seemed more the tapping of a favorite tune on my right breast. Thankfully, he has at least two or three years of medical school left followed by a residency to firm up his skills. Furthermore, his young age made the appointment awkward for us both, and I caught him occasionally smirking. Embarrassed maybe?

3. Dr. C. confirmed clean scans and lack of invasive cancer seen on imaging. She, alongside the rest, is excited and pleased with my significant response to chemotherapy. A total pathological response to chemotherapy!

4. Dennis and I have been married for seven years today. The best time of my life!

Compression Sleeve and Gauntlet

Today was calm, for the most part, except when one of my students came at me with a pair of scissors. Not up for an earlier surgery, please. I have too many commitments this month. Speaking of commitments, I was fitted for a compression sleeve (nylon for your arm) and gauntlet. Sporting these new fashion accessories, I am feeling Michael Jackson-ish. "Just Beat It..." The glove mirrors his style. To prevent a possible lymphedema, I have list of dos and don'ts. Once I consolidate my notes about surgery, radiation and lymphedema, I should log key points. Everything is coming together very quickly now. In the interim, Dennis and I have been busy planning Bryce's 3rd birthday and my "end of chemotherapy-cancer free" party.

Bryce's Third Birthday

This entry comes after a day of needed rest from Bryce's memorable 3rd birthday. A perfect day, completely perfect! The weather was spot-on for a barbeque; there was no shortage of food, and everyone had tons of fun in the huge bounce house that Dennis and I rented for the party. At one point Bryce and his friend, Gregory, were tackling each other between telling jokes – gibberish for the adult mind, hysterics for today's youth. Bryce had fifteen or twenty friends come. Some children were from music class while others were from school, and a fair amount were children of our friends. What a joy! He was happy and proud to have his friends over. Six hundred pictures later (592 to be exact), a caravan of presents, loads of laughs and a missing cake, the day could not have been better.

Today will always be one of those special moments, part of my scrapbook of treasured memories. So many thanks are needed to those who have continued to support us through this journey: the laughs, tears, excitement and hesitation. I never imagined the immense strength I would gain from family and friends and especially, from Dennis and Bryce. So yes, this was a perfect day, completely perfect in every way.

Lists

My surgery became real when I received notification from the "Office of Dr. Q" regarding *pre-op* instructions. Some of these instructions included no aspirin, no vitamin E and no eating or drinking after midnight. Pre-testing is scheduled for Wednesday, and my post-op visit has been arranged for a week and a half after surgery. After the bilateral mastectomy, I have yet another list of instructions for care. My life is full of lists these days but soon enough, the biggest item of my agenda: to be cancer free, will be checked off. A huge weight off my shoulders!

A Week Away

My bilateral mastectomy is one week away. (I decided on a prophylactic left mastectomy to reduce future risk of a possible left breast cancer.) Honestly, I am a bit anxious – mostly about the anesthesia piece of surgery, not the surgery itself ironically. Fortunately, I will meet the anesthesiologist tomorrow to discuss questions I may have.

Locked In

A roller coaster of emotion is the theme of today. Earlier on, I was in hysterics when a student shared his rendition of wig making. He reported, "Okay, wigs are made of cotton that gets strung out. Or sometimes wig makers use real hair. If I knew someone with a wig, I would take their hair and run." Needless to say, I did not tell him that I wore a wig. I could envision him frantically running down the halls while my baldness and I hid from civilization. Later on, this gleeful spirit and optimism came to a halt when suddenly I developed a tsunami of emotion around the anesthesia portion of my surgery. All the words in the world do not seem to lift this irrational fear, the fear of being "locked-in." I am fearful that I will feel the pain of surgery, but not be able to physically articulate these concerns to the surgeon. When I mentioned this to the anesthesiologist, she looked at me like I had four heads. But thankfully, I will be drugged and relaxed enough to not even realize my falling asleep for the operation, or so she says. Finally, this emotional ride subsided, and I returned back to the sauna I call home. It is so hot in here! How do people live without central air conditioning? I will never know. In the evening, Bryce and Dennis returned home from school and then, we had dinner. The night ended with bath time and books, sweating and complaining.

Update:

1. The heating and plumbing company was going to come out this afternoon, and I did not check the messages. Perfect, just perfect!

Heart Tests

Today was my last day of work, and what a crazy one! In the morning, work proceeded as expected until late morning. Around that time, I received a phone call at home and on my cell from the doctor who had booked an afternoon echocardiogram appointment. What?! On an earlier scan, there was mild fluid on my heart called pericardial effusion, which was probably the result of chemotherapy. But yesterday, my EKG was unremarkable. So for what reason did I have this test ordered? Not sure. Assuming this was a standard precaution going into surgery, I did as I was told and arrived for the appointment. The echocardiogram lasted about a half hour. Though, I am not entirely positive of this time duration since I fell asleep on the table. This again confirms my ability to doze anywhere. While the test proceeded without a hitch, and the fluid essentially resolved around my heart, the drive home was not as smooth, literally! My navigation took me up a road, which was unquestionably, the most hazardous part of my day. The road was reduced to one lane secondary to the "craters" on the other side. At one point, I was sure a tow truck would need to assist me. Thankfully I made it in one piece, though I had my quandaries. Mind you, this was also a dirt road, which did not make matters easier. Neither here nor there, I was on my way home soon enough. While driving, I received a phone call to inform me that my compression sleeve and gauntlet had arrived. I turned my CRV around, avoided the treacherous road and trucked back to the medical supply store for these new beige fashion accessories. At last, I was on my way home, for real. There is no place like home.

Other than these errands, I connected with an author and breast cancer survivor who shared words of wisdom. It was comforting to talk with someone who had been in my shoes.

There is No Place Like Home

Tonight, my plans include relaxation, meditation and yoga. At the moment, I am enjoying carrot ginger soup while simultaneously typing. Over one hundred days since the beginning of this adventure, six chemotherapy infusions, more doctors' appointments than I can count, five healing treatments and five bottles of mangosteen juice, I am on my way. Surgery is extremely early at the wee hour of 5:30. My aunt will stay the night to help with Bryce since Dennis and I have to go at the crack of dawn.

A Day Away

Special thanks are extended to family and friends for being with me each step of the way. The sentiments, phone calls, emails, text messages and cards are all appreciated. While I have not been able to field everyone's calls (there have been lots!), I am blessed that an abundance of folks have me in their thoughts and prayers. I hope to write tomorrow before surgery, an optimistic goal. The surgery should take about two and a half hours. And, it is likely that I will be out of the hospital after a day or two. I am unsure how I will be feeling about visitors, but I hope to be up for the company.

My Hero

It is Dennis here. I have been tasked with making sure that the notes Lisa took throughout the day get recorded in her journal tonight. I'll get to it, but first a quick word.

There's a shortage of people to look up to. The world feels crustier and meaner every day. I hate watching the news; I hate reading the paper, and I even hate walking through a crowded mall seeing how people treat each other. This is all Lisa's fault. I'd probably not even notice how miserable so many people are if I did not have the most positive and entirely authentic "nice guy(girl)" living with me every day. It breaks my heart that she had to go through this ordeal, but it's given her a chance to impress and humble me all over again. There is no one like Lisa. I'm lucky to have found such a great wife and mother for my son. I'm in awe of how she has handled the past few months. Amazing. There's nothing she can't do...

...and that's why I'm leaving these dishes in the sink for when she gets home.

Pre surgery Commentary (from Lisa)
Here I am, sitting in the pre-surgical area
awaiting my bilateral mastectomy. This
room reminds me of a horse stable with it
being so close to the next one. Of course, it is
far more sanitary. All my vitals were good,
and the nurse who came to explain the
procedure says I may wake up with oxygen
and massaging boots. Sweet – massaging!
Just a moment ago, I took Valium so my
writing may quickly go downhill. The
mastectomy will start about 7:30 and should
last about two and a half hours. By afternoon
time, I hope to be out of recovery. Onward
and upward!

Post-Surgical Notes
Here I am, sitting in room 500 having just
undergone a bilateral mastectomy with right
axillary node dissection. I feel okay
considering I recently had a shot of
morphine. Besides that, the surgery went
well. Dr. Q got everything, and I speak with
him again tomorrow. I was in the operating
room until about noon followed by recovery
until about 2:30. Prior to surgery, I had
heartfelt conversations with both nurses and
doctors to reassure me that the anesthesia
would be administered flawlessly. It is
seldom that a "locked-in" situation arises and
when it does, it is seen mostly in folks who
consume large amounts of barbiturates,

alcohol, or, in trauma patients. I certainly do not fit those categories even despite the drugs I have done this year. After a visit with the anesthesiologist, I saw Dr. Q who stated, "Beauty is in your eyes, not your feet" when I referenced treating my ugly feet to a spa pedicure over the weekend.

Additional Updates:

1. I will be discharged in one day.

2. The swelling in my chest resembles an A-cup.

3. Got milk? I do! I have what seems like strawberry milk in two bottles: one on each side, which I periodically empty.

• Dennis again. One last note about Lisa's day that is just so typical Lisa. At the end of the night, she went to press the button in her right hand that summons the nurse but instead pressed the button in her left hand that gave her a shot of morphine. She let out an "Ah shoot", which is her version of a swear and laid back for some zzz's.

Percocet + Lisa = Very Sleepy

I am loopy and craving popsicles. While in the hospital, there was an endless parade of doctors, nurses, insurance representatives and other medical professionals who monitored my progress. All had positive reports. While there, I learned how to empty drains, clean piping and change gauze pads. Across my chest, I have two horizontal incisions. After getting the green light from Dr. Q, my surgeon, Dennis packed my bags and drove us home. I am so tired. Percocet + Lisa = Very Sleepy.

Day One Home

This whole ordeal seems like a strange dream. I closed my eyes after hearing the initial diagnosis and now, I open my eyes and am cancer free.

Percocet really knocks me out. Most of the time, I sleep – company or no company. I also do my touchdown and itsy-bitsy spider exercises to improve range of motion in my arms, particularly the right one. Dennis takes care of household responsibilities (i.e. trash, dishes). In the midst of today's events, the visiting nurse also arrived to change my dressing and pads. The pads were dry with no sign of infection. She will return daily until my surgical follow-up appointment. Overall, I am moving around fairly well, reading and sleeping (as I described earlier). The house is so quiet with Bryce at school; I miss him.

True Love, Surely

It is late morning, and I just awoke from a peaceful catnap on the couch. Dennis and Bryce went to a water park, and although I wanted to join in the fun, my current physical state suggested otherwise. Being home all day with no distractions is quite the change. Consequently, I have been doing a lot of reading since I do not watch much television. Maybe later, I will take a short walk when Dennis returns from the park.

Additional Updates:

1. Last night, Dennis helped me take a sponge bath. I cannot get wet from my waist upward due to incisions and drains. Dennis also changes my gauze daily. Even though I look gross from waist up, I am thrilled to be healthy. But seriously, my chest resembles the impression of two craters, one on each side. On the left I also have bunched

skin, which will promote better reconstruction. But now, it looks ridiculous. And somehow, my husband still says I look great. Ha! I am making a point to call his eye doctor immediately; we have to get his prescription renewed. True love, surely.

To Be Continued ... (later today)

Once again, I rise from another nap. Effects of Percocet, I think. During my rest, I had the craziest dream: I called 9-1-1 on a little boy lurking outside my house, only to find out that he was afraid of cats and wanted to come inside. Dreams never make sense. Anyway, in the short time that I have been awake, both Edible Arrangements and UPS came with surprises. I should rest more often since I wake up to flowers and candy.

Words of Wisdom:

1. The greatest thing in the world is not so much where we are, but in which direction we are moving.
   – *O. Holmes*

2. On not waiting: As it says in the Bible, "if you wait until the wind

and the weather are just right, you will never plant anything and never harvest anything." There is no better time to begin than today.

3. Good survivors aren't immune to fear. They know what's happening, and it does scare the living shit out of them. It's all a question of what to do next.
    – *L. Gonzales*

4. If fate throws a knife at you, there are two ways of catching it – by the blade and by the handle.
    – Ancient Proverb

    I am catching my fate by the handle thanks to a positive attitude and excellent traveling companions: Dennis, Bryce, family and friends.

Not One, Not Two but Three

Not one, not two, but three deliveries today.

Regarding recovery, it was a bit "touch n' go." I felt nauseous for a good portion of the day, probably secondary to Percocet. Therefore, I did not eat too much. After one of my several naps, Dennis, Bryce and I attempted to go for a car ride, which did not pan out. About half way there, I asked Dennis to turn around and then slept a few more hours in my cozy bed.

Good news: I have better range of motion in my arms. My left arm is almost back to normal, and my right is a bit behind that. Each day, I do my arm exercises in between dosages of pain medicine. Dennis is an exceptional help since I cannot do much on my own. However I am proud to say I dressed myself in jean capris and a button down shirt for the first time since before surgery.

Additional Updates:

1. I put on my rings for the first time since before surgery; swelling has subsided.

2. I do not have feeling under my right arm. Permanent, I believe.

Doing Better

Secondary to nausea, constipation is the worst. Thankfully, Senocot-S and hot green tea do the trick. Of everything I could complain about, constipation is on top of my list. Ugh!

Medical Updates:

1. I have tingling in my right arm, which the doctors said would happen.

2. Nausea has subsided. I switched to Motrin for pain medicine since Percocet is too hard-core.

3. My next appointment with the surgical oncologist to review pathology of remaining cancer, if any, is soon.

I Am ...

CANCER FREE! I waited a long while to write these words. At the start of my journaling, I wanted *cancer free* to be the happy conclusion. But what I realize now is that this is the beginning of a new chapter in my life. I have been given a second opportunity to live more fully, experience all my desires, love deeply, laugh loudly and appreciate everything. The last bit is crucial. Appreciate everything.

The petty squabbles and silly worries are trivial in the grand scheme of what is really worthwhile to spend your energy. In a sense, this cancer has been a deranged blessing to remind me of these points and to make each day count. The tireless support, unconditional love, supportive friendship and undying compassion made this journey what it is. This entry is really the beginning.

Cancer Free

My aunt came to visit today, and we relaxed at a local orchard and enjoyed delicious ice cream. It was a perfect combination of enjoying the outdoors while still resting. I am a bit achy, but with my chin up. Last night, I required the assistance of Ativan to sleep since back sleeping is not for me. Drains on the left, drains on the right, tubes up the middle. It is a labyrinth of apparatus. Not to mention pillows in the middle of the bed to elevate my right arm. But really, what a small price to pay for health! I am on cloud nine.

Quotes

Bryce Quote of the Day # 1 – "Will the doctors put your boobs back?"

Today, I had an appointment with my surgical oncologist, and he was thrilled with the positive response to chemotherapy, excellent scans and a perfect surgery. Dr. Q. says, "I can tell you with 99.9% certainty that you are completely cured." With tears in his eyes he says, "I will wear your lime green bandana every time I go sailing and think of you. God Bless You." A nurse shared that I was her first patient from start to finish; the entire office was in tears of joy, an uplifting visit.

Despite my sheer happiness, I continue to have these damn drains. Coming up, I meet with both my radiation and medical oncologists. All is good, and I am beginning the development of a *healing plan* to maintain balance in my life.

Bryce Quote of the Day # 2 (on going to sleep) – "The only time I should call for you is if the roof is caving in, my belly hurts or my bed falls apart." What a ham!

Thoughts

Last night, I slept like a baby for the first time in a while, and I am able to cut back marginally on pain medicine. For the first time in many months, I do not feel like a drug user. The visiting nurse just left, and I am now off to hours of reading and draining. Wednesdays and Thursdays are so quiet with my being home alone but luckily, today, I received two girly movies in the mail from my best friend, Nancy.

Additional Updates:

1. My hair is growing in jet-black.

2. I have resumed shaving with consistency.

3. My nails have yet to grow out. Now, they have lifted off the nail beds.

4. My left breast is wrinkled like an old lady's and the right side is concave like a canyon.

Draining and Draining

Today, the visiting nurse arrived and alerted to me to minor irritation on the left drainage site. When Melissa (the nurse) was here, she reeked of smoke. I didn't think she would smoke (1) being a nurse and (2) being an extremely health conscious person so I refrained from saying anything but was so curious about the ghastly stench. Then, Melissa shared that she had just come from another patient's home where the patient, a recent survivor of bladder cancer, caused by the carcinogens of smoking, was puffing away. When asked if he understood the implications caused by smoking he replied, "sure, but the docs gave me a new bladder so

I must have another fifty years on this one. I'll be 100 by that time." I was in awe but then again, look at me – ah! It doesn't pay to be good sometimes; therefore, I am now going to drink myself into oblivion while eating fatty foods. Afterwards, I went to the store but arranged my outfit a million different ways before leaving to cover these annoying drains. It is lucky I made it there before closing.

A funny story: Bryce was watching a children's program and at one point, one of the characters (a notepad) was singing a song about her being flat. The beat was catchy, and I bopped to the tune when Dennis asked me, "Is that your new theme song?" Very funny. Though, I am as flat as the notepad in the show.

Additional Updates:

1. I have a shadow of jet-black hair.

2. Upcoming doctor appointments will determine need for radiation.

3. My surgeon removed thirteen nodes, all cancer free.

4. Herceptin resumes.

Champagne Worthy

Despite a champagne worthy response to chemotherapy as my radiation oncologist stated, I will still require radiation. Twenty-eight treatments to be exact: Monday through Friday every morning through the summer months. Dr. C. informed me that even though my surgical pathology was excellent, her recommendation to radiate was based on several factors: my age, initial diagnosis and type of breast cancer. The complete cure will involve sanitation of my skin, and I am fully on-board. The daily sessions will be interesting to finagle with Bryce even though treatments are only about fifteen minutes in length. Speaking of Bryce, Dennis and I have decided to transform our extra room into a playroom. Shelving is still needed but so far, looking good.

After my visit with Dr. C, I traveled from the University Campus (where I enrolled in medical school) to the Memorial Campus (where Nurse Diane removed my left drain). While I was psyched to lose one of my faithful companions, the other is still holding tight,

which now substantiates a short course of
antibiotics. My goal is to remove the other
drain by the time my brother gets married,
which is soon. Though it only figures that the
drains are coming out just as I learned a way
to mask the turkey-baster looking apparatus:
hide them under a dress. Genius!
Regardless, I am happy to see them go so I
can sleep more comfortably. Back sleeping is
such a task, and I am not a happy camper
without adequate sleep. By extension,
neither is my husband. I moan and groan all
night at the result of not catching required
zzzz's. However with the left drain now out, I
shall be able to sleep like a baby.

After these doctor appointments, I ventured
to Rhode Island for a dress fitting. Emily, the
seamstress, is adding boobs to my dress as
part of the alteration. Essentially, she is
placing two shoulder pads into each cup. The
usage of shoulder pads is back in full swing. I
should have saved them years ago. Who
would have thought they'd have another
purpose? That being said, after Emily
finished pinning me into my princess gown,
like Bryce refers, I felt surprised to look
normally endowed. A job well done! The
adventure through Rhode Island started at

the dress fitting and continued with a lovely visit with mom, a warm cup of tea with my future sister-in-law, Jennifer, and a panicked visit at the supermarket. That's right, panicked! After purchasing costly but worthwhile soaps, lotions and sunscreen, I am at the register when I suddenly realize I misplaced my keys. So instead of supporting my obvious panic with reassuring comments, the cordial man at the check-out says, "You know miss, in my youth, I used to hot-wire cars. We will get you home." That is one solution, I suppose, probably not the best one nor one that I would voluntarily choose. But hey, he was trying to lighten the situation. Long story short, I found my keys (in my pocketbook no less) and returned back to my car, expensive groceries in hand. A similar event happened this morning when Dennis raced out the door to work. Bryce was settled in his car seat; Dennis placed the key into his ignition, and the thing fell to pieces. A computer chip here, a plastic piece there and he, powerless to stop it. Dennis and I are both meant to hang home and save gas.

Interesting Updates:

1. I have limited sensation at the incision site and around my armpit. It feels sort of like the injection of local anesthesia in that there is pressure, but no pain. At one point, I relaxed my arms to the side and thought, "did I forget to remove gauze from under my arm?" I looked and discovered that I was actually feeling my own skin.

2. I have Herceptin therapy now (11 more rounds, every three weeks) and an upcoming doctor appointment with my medical oncologist, Dr. E.

3. Jet-black hair is still growing, but not very fast.

4. I washed my wig and compression sleeve last night.

5. Even though I have not taken a full shower in close to a month (gross!), partial showers are doing the trick. And better than that, I can do it myself now.

Room Five

Here I reside in room five, once again, for chemotherapy. This time however, there will be no side effects including nausea, hair loss and exhaustion, and I will be done in record time. What a change from the previous regime, which by the way, I feel blessed to have had. Dr. E. was overjoyed and stated that my response to chemotherapy was her best news, as of late. This statement was humbling in itself and shortly after, I came across a patient in the waiting area who had Stage 4 Breast Cancer since it spread to another part of her body. This woman had a 4-year-old son, and my heart ached for her. After I learned of this, I felt horrible to have been so exuberant with flowers for my doctors as well as smiles from ear to ear that I am cancer free. While of course I am thrilled for my outcome, my heart deeply ached for this girl, and I was speechless. A tinge of sadness but the expression of my feelings – positive and otherwise, is therapeutic. In moving forward however, here is abbreviated version of my upcoming treatment.

1. Herceptin – every three weeks for ten more treatments.

2. Twenty-eight daily radiation treatments and a possible boost to the scar.

3. Zometa – two times a year (for bone health). This will be given only if "pre-menopausal" Lisa does not return.

4. Five years of Tamoxifen.

A Perfect Analogy

Today, my medical oncologist had a lengthy conversation with me. Occasionally, I am nervous about recurrence. She stated, "If you own a house, you have fire insurance. However each time you leave the house, you do not worry that your house will burn down. Recovering from cancer is similar in the sense that an excellent response to chemotherapy was had with a cancer free outcome, and excellent research-based treatment was provided with perfect success. Confidence in your health is key." This is true.

Grounded

The drain on my right is still in place with no sign of near-future removal. After speaking with Nurse Diane, she tells me that the next "call back" day is Wednesday. Of no surprise, it seems I am doing too much. Consequently, the doctor tells me to lay low so fluids will subside, and I can bid farewell to the right drain.

Other than that, all is well. I got concert tickets for my birthday, and my brother is getting married Sunday. In the interim, I will have another day of rest and relaxation. My hair is still growing, wispy and soft. And, I need to shave my legs.

You're Expecting, Right?

All is well and no, I am not expecting. Expecting a grand wedding this weekend – yes, but a baby, not so much. How shocked I was when a cashier at the local grocery store asked of my due date. She graciously offered to put my groceries on the conveyor belt because "you will need your rest soon..." Wow! I mean, yes, I do have a little belly and next to no chest (which consequently accentuates my belly, but come on, I am certainly not waddling). The sight of a waddling woman is the only time, if you ask at all, to inquire of someone's pregnancy. The whole situation was funny though, if she only knew. I better live on the blackberries growing in my backyard for a few weeks. Evidently, I am expecting or playing the role very well.

Apart from having a baby, the other fabulous news is that my right drain was removed today. What a sigh of relief! On the way out of the hospital, I saw my surgical oncologist, Dr. Q., who gave Bryce and me a hug. I am blessed to be around such loving and brilliant professionals who saved my life. For that, I am eternally grateful. But also, the thoughtfulness of family and friends has been paramount. For example, my aunt treated me to a lovely spa pedicure in preparation for my brother's wedding. That same day, another dear friend came to visit. She is a survivor of breast cancer by seventeen years and recently, she and her husband started a business selling beautiful sterling silver healing bracelets. They are incredible, and she gave me one with a few charms. In typical fashion, Bryce did not go without. We now have a few more books to add to his growing collection.

Wedding Bells

Beautiful, beautiful and more beautiful! Every detail was thoroughly planned from the programs and flowers to the decorations and dresses. At the reception, there was even a photo booth. Jennifer and Eddy both dressed the part perfectly, and Bryce was so handsome. Throughout the weekend, I remained in positive spirits with occasional fatigue. I wore my compression sleeve and glove as much as possible but honestly, the momentum of the weekend kept me driving forward with a cheek-to-cheek smile. My friend, Nancy, came to the wedding reception to watch Bryce in the evening.

Additional Updates:

1. Dennis tells me that in a week or two, my hair will be like a short hair cut. Suspect.

2. I took my first full shower.

3. I also exercised for the first time since before surgery.

You Got a Tattoo?

Yes! That's an affirmative. While I would

have desired something a bit cooler like, well, I don't know. Regardless, I sport six small freckle-size radiation tattoos to mark where beams will pass. Dr. C. will radiate the chest and nodal area for a total of twenty-eight daily treatments at 7:30 each morning. By my calculations, I will be finished on my husband's birthday. The pre-radiation CT scan revealed no nodes of concern. With that said, Dr. C. plans to fuse the original CT scans with those of today to guarantee that questionable areas were removed by surgery or melted away by chemotherapy. At our next appointment, we will review this information. In the interim, radiation will be administered with my arms placed above my head, and head to be turned to the left. This will clear a margin for the beam to meet with the right side of my chest, nodal areas and neck region. I should expect a "razzle-red" skin color from the beams. Dr. C. told me, "in all likelihood, you are already completely cured." Thank you! Thank you!

My Birthday

I turned thirty-two. It was a splendid day, and I appreciate birthdays so much more now. After a series of jingle calls and delicious breakfast served by my totally outstanding husband, Dennis, Bryce and I enjoyed summer fun blowing bubbles and playing in Bryce's sandbox. Tomorrow, we are off to New Hampshire for a quick jaunt before radiation begins. Have to squeeze in some fun these days – lots of appointments.

New Hampshire

Swimming, hiking and boating were highlights of our trip. I never knew I had such adventurous boys. At one point, the three of us took a chairlift to the mountain summit and hiked throughout the rocky terrain. Totally exhausted, Bryce incessantly asked Dennis, "Can you pick me up?" Cute. It was an exciting little vacation away with my family.

A Full Agenda

After a few fun-filled days, it is back to reality. I met with my radiation skincare nurse, Cindy. She too was extremely knowledgeable and outlined the expectations of radiation. The top ten ideas follow.

1. Radiation will be given by external beam. A machine (similar to CT scan or MRI) will pivot around the upper half of my body with an "arm" that

directs radiation to the chest wall and supra-clavicular lymph nodes (neck region). The entire visit from start to finish will be twenty minutes, but the radiation itself will last between five and eight minutes. Once a week, I meet with my radiation oncologist.

2. No jewelry, band-aids, powder, lotion or deodorant allowed in the area where radiation will be provided. Crystal body deodorant is okay.

3. Side effects include fatigue (maybe) and redness in the area where beams pass.

4. No razor shaving under the right arm. Buzzing is fine (not that there is much hair).

5. All natural soaps and lotions are required.

6. No sunscreen allowed. No other products with aluminum, zinc or titanium are to be used.

7. No swimming in chlorinated water, particularly, and ocean water is also discouraged.

8. No hot water bottles, heating pads or ice packs can be applied to the treated area.

9. It is preferred to abstain from wearing a bra through the radiation treatment period. Darn it! My huge boobs are going to be so sore.

10. Sunscreen containing an SPF of 30 (after radiation is completed) must be applied daily a full year following this treatment. In treatment, direct exposure to the sun must be minimal.

My First Radiation Treatment

6:30 in the morning – Bzzzz! Bzzzz! Bzzzz! At the all-too-early sound of my alarm, I rolled out of bed and ventured to Worcester for my first day of radiation. Since I did not have to tend to hair or make-up, I quickly dressed, snatched blueberries from the fridge and water from the cooler and hopped in the car by 6:45. I arrived to the hospital by 7:20, parked and descended to the basement, where radiation took place. The entire process was seamless. At the entrance, I scanned my self check-in card and then went to the changing room. Everything from the waist up was removed, and I wrapped myself in two hospital gowns: one open in the front and the other open in the back. Then, I lockered my belongings and proceeded to the waiting room.

Promptly at 7:30, the technician summoned me to the radiation table where I lounged in the expected radiation position. The "arm" traveled around my body making a clicking sound while simultaneously shooting beams of radiation through the right side chest wall and neck region. After a few rounds of radiation were emitted, the technician came back to place the bolus atop my chest. The bolus looked like a 9x9 white square ice pack, which I learned, attracts radiation closer to the skin. By 7:40, I was finished. Soon after, I met with the doctor who took a baseline glance at my skin. A-okay. By 8:00, I was off to see Bryce.

Monotony

The monotony of radiation is interesting. The daily schedule follows.

6:30 Ring, ring! Rise and Shine.

6:45 Drive to radiation, jive to music and enjoy blueberries with yogurt.

7:17 Pull into the hospital garage and find my "reserved parking spot." The garage is always empty at this time and the same spot is always available.

7:20-7:27 Walk to the doctor's past the same two medical students reading and drinking coffee – Jim and Nadine (yes, I read their tags); head to the basement and self-scan myself into the appointment. A lovely couple waits in the sitting area. I proceed to locker seventeen, grab two johnnies – one for my front and one for my back, quickly robe into this fashionable attire, toss my shirt into the locker and "advance to go," I mean to the waiting area.

7:30 The therapist meets me with a morning smile. Radiation begins. I study the numbers on the screen, read my name and statistics. After I am aligned on the table, a set of beeps occurs; the radiation therapist comes back to the room, places a metal shield in the machine and bolus atop my chest for another succession of beeps. This repeats one more time except for the next series, she switches out the metal shield for another and moves the bolus about two inches to the left. All is said and done by 7:40. I dress in my street clothes and exit the office. I pass the same folks on my way out.

7:47 After validating my parking, I am on route home and ready for the day by 8:15.

Mama, Where'd your Boobs Go?

Oh no! Bryce is just three and already asking about boobs. He and I were telling stories before bed and in typical inquisitive fashion, one question after another ended in this comment.

Anyway, the monotony continues; however, I am nearly halfway through radiation. No side effects barring a little pinkness in the area where treatment occurs. I met with my doctor today, and all is perfect.

My hair is very short and very dark. *Very* is the operative word. I feel hesitant to be in public with my hair so short; however, many are encouraging me to do so. An aside: my wig shifts constantly because of this underlying hair layer.

Health

I feel healthy, started exercising and shed a few pounds gained by steroid usage during chemotherapy. My skin is a light shade of pink, nothing striking. I read that drinking Eleuthero Root tea is beneficial in counteracting the detrimental effects of radiation and increasing the numbers of immune cells. The taste is tolerable. Interestingly, results of a recent Australian study showed that men and women who took Eleuthero presented with 13% strength gains in the pectoral muscles and 15% gain in their biceps. But for me, the simple results to maintain healthy skin cells and immunities are fine.

On another note, I cannot wear a bra to reduce skin irritation and boast a hairy right armpit since (for the same reason). But all is well. Lately, I have also become a hat-wearing enthusiast. I have three: green, pink and yellow. Despite early runs to Worcester, I enjoy summer day trips with friends and family. I visited the beach several times (umbrella and hat in hand), went to a baseball game, out for ice cream, dancing and the movies. Really, I cannot complain. I continue to eat healthy, whole foods as well as heal by setting small monthly well-being goals for myself. Just yesterday, I was speaking with my sister-in-law and caught myself saying, "This cancer was sort of a good thing for me. While I would not wish this on anyone or myself again, it really taught me to appreciate life. My mom always says "everything happens for a reason" and while I *believed* this, I never really *understood* it until now.

Seven More Treatments

Radiation is dwindling down with only seven more treatments culminating on my husband's 32nd birthday. All is status quo. My radiation oncologist rates the irritation of my skin at a one or two on a scale of ten, which is excellent. In the morning, I slather on radiation cream and in the evening, I douse in more cream.

Firsts

I wore my short hair for the *first* time when going out to eat. Of course, a hat was included in the deal. And also, I ran for the *first* time in nine months.

Today, I also had an appointment with Dr. Q, my surgical oncologist. He is impressed by my recovery and scheduled a follow up appointment in one year. One year! I also made an appointment to meet with the plastic surgeon. Reconstruction is planned for six months out, which will allow my skin to heal.

In the midst of firsts and appointments, I continue to read about nutrition. Below are five informative thoughts for a general audience. Keeping it light and fluffy, of course!

1. Countries with more telephone poles have higher incidence of heart disease and many other diseases. Strange!!

2. Hot dogs – the worst kind of processed meat. Besides containing additives like nitrites, hot dogs can be made out of ground-up lips, snouts, spleens, tongues, throats and other "variety meats." Appetizing?

3. Breast cancer is associated with animal fat intake but not with plant fat. Furthermore, there is a very impressive relationship between dietary fat and breast cancer.

4. High Protein/Low Carbohydrate Diets
    – Sure, there can be weight loss
    initially due to restricted caloric
    intake but during further exploration
    of this diet type, side effects of
    constipation, bad breath, headache,
    hair loss and increased bleeding were
    also documented.

5. Everything in food works together to
    create health or disease. So eat well!

Radiation – Completed

After 8000+ "rads" to the right chest wall and
supra-clavicular region, I now have sunburn
symbolizing the culmination of my breast
cancer treatment. This is another reason to
celebrate. Speaking of celebration, Dennis'
birthday was yesterday, and we were treated
to lawn seats at Fenway Park in Boston,
Massachusetts. It was the best. I could throw
a stone to first base; we were *that* close.

Future Plans:

1. Eight more Herceptin infusions.

2. Tamoxifen, an oral medication.

3. Visits with doctors every three to four

months for the few years; every six months thereafter.

So many people have taken time out of their busy lives to keep track of mine. I am forever grateful and overjoyed.

Plan for Plastic Surgery

Contrary to former beliefs, I do not have enough stomach fat to make even an A-cup so my initial tummy-tuck aspirations will not be the way to go. On the contrary, the plastic surgeon will stretch muscle flaps from my back to my chest, suture the muscle in place and then insert a silicone implant. Prior to the implant placement, an expander will serve to *expand* the skin to my desired size preference. This could be fun!

Looking Back, Looking Ahead

I have learned more lessons in one year than I have in my entire life. I have learned to love deeply, live well, laugh often, appreciate everything and make each day count. Overall, I am confident in my health; I eat well, exercise and take supplements. I enjoy reading about nutrition and ways to strengthen my entire self: physically, mentally and spiritually. But most of all, I enjoy my family and friends, especially my husband, Dennis and son, Bryce. They have always been the driving force behind my will to beat breast cancer. I love them both more than words can say.

When writing this memoir, I wanted to someday inspire another, as many have inspired me. If I touch the life of just one future survivor, then I feel successful in giving back and making a difference, which is what I hoped my writing would do.

To the Reader: A Final Thought

Maryann Wolf writes, "wisdom begins where that of the author ends, and we would like to have him give us all the answers, while all he can do is give us desires." What are your desires?

Onward and Upward,
Lisa

Appendix

Lisa's Lists

A. Recipes

These recipes are a select few of my favorites. Family and friends have passed these along to me, and I have modified them to my liking. The original sources for these dishes are unknown.

1. Apple Pizza

Ingredients:

½ cup ricotta cheese

3 tbsp minced red onion

½ cup diced red, yellow or green peppers

Multi-grain pizza crust

1 Honey Crisp apple, cored and thinly sliced

½ cup jarred sweet red pepper, thinly sliced

¾ cup shredded mozzarella cheese

Directions:

Preheat oven to 425° F. In a small bowl, combine ricotta cheese, onion and peppers; mix well. Spread on pizza crust. Layer apple and red pepper on top of ricotta mixture. Sprinkle with mozzarella. Bake between 9 and 11 minutes or until cheese melts and pizza is heated through. This makes approximately 4 servings.

2. Banana Berry Smoothie

Ingredients:

1 frozen banana, sliced into chunks

¼ cup blueberries

¼ cup raspberries

1-½ cups milk

½ tsp vanilla extract

¼ tsp almond extract

Pinch of ground cinnamon

Directions:

In a blender, combine all ingredients except cinnamon. Blend 20 seconds or more until smooth. Pour into glasses and sprinkle ground cinnamon on top. This makes approximately 2 servings.

3. Eggless Vegetarian Quiche

Ingredients:

1 cup cauliflower (cut in flowerets)

½ cup sliced carrots

¼ cup sliced zucchini

¾ cup water-packed artichoke hearts

12 oz. sour cream

½ cup Parmesan cheese
1 cup grated Monterey Jack cheese
2 tablespoons cornstarch
3 teaspoons of olive oil
½ teaspoon crushed, or powdered garlic
¼ teaspoon black pepper
Pinch of turmeric

Crust:
1 ½ cups multi-grain flour
½ cup melted butter
1/3 cup Parmesan cheese
3 tablespoons water

Directions:
Blend flour, cheese and butter. Texture will resemble wet sand. Add water a little at a time. Pat the mixture on bottom and along sides of 9-inch quiche pan. Bake at 400° F for 8 minutes.

In a fry skillet, heat oil and add garlic. Add cauliflower and carrots. Stir until they are evenly coated. Cover and cook for 10 minutes over medium heat, stirring occasionally. Add zucchini and cook 5 more minutes.

In large bowl, combine sour cream, cornstarch, pepper and turmeric. Add Parmesan cheese and ½ cup Monterey Jack cheese. Fold in vegetables and artichoke hearts. Pour into quiche pan and top with remaining Monterey Jack cheese. Bake at 400° F for 40 minutes or until the edges of the quiche are dark and the center is slightly golden. Allow the quiche to set about 30 minutes before cutting and serving.

4. <u>Quinoa Stuffed Pepper</u>

Ingredients:
1 onion, diced
2 garlic cloves, minced
2 tablespoons olive oil
1 teaspoon tomato paste
2 cups of diced tomatoes
1 cup cooked Quinoa
1 teaspoon lemon juice
1 tablespoon chopped parsley
1/3 cup feta cheese
Salt and Pepper to taste

Directions:
1. Cook diced onion and 2 cloves of minced garlic in 2 tablespoons olive oil until tender. Add one teaspoon of tomato paste and cook for 2 minutes. Add two cups diced tomatoes; cook 10 minutes more.
2. Fold in 1 cup cooked quinoa, 1 teaspoon lemon juice, 1 tablespoon chopped parsley, 1/3 cup feta cheese and salt/pepper to taste.

3. Pour ½ cup water into a baking dish
   and add 4 halved, seeded red bell
   peppers filled with mixture. Bake
   covered at 400 for 30-40 minutes.
   Add 1/3 cup of feta and broil
   uncovered until cheese is brown.

B. Meditations

A good friend shared these meditations with
me, and I continue to enjoy them.

1. Imagine you are in a beautiful lagoon
   at night. The island is lush with tall,
   tropical trees, shiny green leaves and
   perfumed flowers. The moon is full,
   shining on the deep blue water with
   all its glowing brilliance. There are
   sounds of night birds and the rushing
   sound from a clear, cascading
   waterfall.

   Stand under the waterfall and let the
   water clear all negativity from your
   being. From your head, to your
   shoulders and your arms and your
   chest, then to your stomach and legs.
   Just let it go.

   When you feel completely refreshed,
   swim toward the center of the lagoon,
   where the moonlight is the brightest.
   Suddenly, a large white seashell rises

slowly from the water. Climb aboard the shell and stand with your arms outstretched, absorbing all the moonlight. Let the moonlight energize your entire body, from your head, to your shoulders and your arms and your chest, then to your stomach and legs.

Now bend down to see your reflection on the bright, moonlit water. What does your face look like? What does your hair look like? What does your body look like? If you do not like the person you see, stir the water with your hand until your reflection shows you as a smiling, healthy person who is very, very loved.

Now visualize your family, friends and co-workers. Are they understanding? Are they supportive? If you do not like what you see, stir the water with your hand until you see yourself talking to them and explaining exactly how you wish to be treated.

Dive off the shell with a big splash, swimming underwater in the moonlight. You can see the entire water world quite clearly from the seaweed and coral to the schools of

many tropical fish. When you are
ready to rest, swim to shore and lie
down in the cool, moist grass. Now
open your eyes and feel refreshed.
For the first time in a long time, you
truly feel happy and free! Gone is your
pain, your sadness and your fears. You
can see clearly now and you are in
control.

2. Imagine you are walking through a
    bright, moonlit path in the woods near
    a river, carrying a warm, red blanket, a
    wooden flute and a picnic basket.

    Your feet are crunching on dry, brown
    and yellow leaves and there are
    rabbits and squirrels scampering
    across your path.

    As you walk, you notice that the leaves
    are becoming damper as you get
    closer to the water. Bend down and
    collect twelve of the moist leaves and
    place them inside your basket. You
    will use these later when you are
    ready for releasement.

    Soon you are out of the woods and
    directly facing the rolling river, its
    dark water rushing over the smooth,
    large rocks. The Full Moon shines like

a lunar spotlight on the gentle waves and you are grateful for its comforting brilliance on this dark and cold night.

Find a good spot and spread the blanket on the hard ground. Then place the basket and flute on one end and be seated on the other.

Now open your basket and remove a leaf. Think of a fear that you would like to release at this time. It may be a fear of failure, a fear of heights, a fear of change, a fear of death. No matter what the fear, you are releasing it today.

As you think of your fear, lift the leaf above your head and announce, "I release this fear to the river and to the Universe. It is no longer mine to bear."

Then, toss the leaf into the water and watch your fear float away. Now do this with five more leaves until these fears, too, have floated away.

Now think of all the things you may feel guilty about. Perhaps you feel guilty over something you said, or something you did, or something that

you did not do. You want to release
these guilty feelings too.

Remove a leaf from the basket and lift
it high above your head. Then say
aloud: " I release this guilt to the river
and to the Universe. It is no longer
mine to bear."

Toss this leaf into the water and watch
it until it disappears from view. Then
remove the remaining five leaves from
your basket and repeat this ritual until
all of the leaves have disappeared
down the river.

Now open the basket and remove your
drinking cup and a loaf of hearty,
whole grain bread. Before you eat this
meal of thanksgiving, think of all the
reasons you have to be grateful. Be
grateful for Mother Earth, for her trees
and rivers and oceans and mountains.
Be grateful for the moon and the stars,
the night and the air.

Be grateful for the fish in the waters,
the birds in the skies, the plants and
the animals.

Be grateful for your family, your
friends, your employer, your

employees, your co-workers and your teachers. All that exists have lessons to teach you, and you are grateful for their guidance.

Now dip your cup into the river, which flows with the goodness of clear, clean, drinkable water. Return to the blanket and bless your meal. With each mouthful of bread and each sip of water, you feel more grateful, more satisfied with your life.

Overhead, the Full Moon appears to grow larger and larger as it pours its healing white light upon you. In gratitude, you pick up your flute and play a song of thanks to the heavens.

You are grateful for your life. You are grateful for this day. All your fears and guilt have been removed from your being. All is well.

C. My Cancer-Free Diet

Listed below are a few of the many tips I learned about eating healthier, improving immunity and starving off disease.

1. Limit consumption of refined sugars (cane and beet sugar, corn syrup), bleached flour (white bread/pasta) and vegetable oils (soybean,

sunflower, corn, trans fats). These lower immunities.
2. Reduce consumption of red meat and avoid processed pork products.
3. Enjoy multigrain bread (made from wheat with at least three other cereals such as oatmeal, rye, flaxseeds, etc.)
4. Savor fruit in its natural state, particularly blueberries, cherries and raspberries, which help to regulate blood sugar.
5. Bulk up on Omega – 3s that are found in organic products from grass-fed animals. These help the body fight disease.
6. Choose green tea as a drink of choice, a powerful antioxidant and detoxifier.
7. Munch on Brazil Nuts. These are rich in Selenium, another powerful antioxidant.
8. Season with Turmeric, a powerful natural anti-inflammatory.

"Food" for Thought ...
Michael Pollan states in <u>Food Rules</u>, "it's not food if it arrived through the window of your car." A balanced diet includes *real* food, mostly plants and not too much. After all, you are what you eat.

D. Books

1. Campbell, T. C., Campbell, T. M., *The China Study: the most comprehensive study of nutrition ever conducted and the startling implications for diet, weight loss and long-term health* (Texas: Benbella Books, 2006).

2. Gavigan, C., *Healthy Child, Healthy World: creating a cleaner, greener, safer home* (New York: Penguin Group, 2009).

3. Peale, N., *Positive Thinking Everyday: an inspiration for each day of the year* (New York: Simon & Schuster, 1993).

4. Pollan, M., *Food Rules: an eater's manual* (New York: Penguin Group, 2009).

5. Roizen, M., Oz, M., *You Staying Young: the owner's manual for extending your warranty* (New York: Simon & Schuster, 2007).

6. Schreiber, D. *Anticancer: a new way of life* (New York: Penguin Group, 2009).

7. Silver, J., *Super Healing: the clinically proven plan to maximize recovery from illness or injury* (New York: Holtzbrinck, 2007).

E. The "Chemo-Care" Package

While each case of breast cancer is different, undergoing chemotherapy is no easy task for anyone. The following items were the "must-haves" during my treatment:

1. Wasa Crackers – This snack was wonderful to keep nausea at bay.
2. Bioténe Mouthwash – I used this product daily to prevent mouth sores.
3. Tea Tree Oil – This was another daily necessity, which I used on my cuticles to prevent infection.
4. Colorful bandanas, of course!
5. Unscented hand and body lotions were excellent for my dry skin.
6. Relaxing music and meditation DVDs hit the spot.
7. Uplifting books were the perfect accessory.

F. Quotes

"Nothing great was ever achieved without enthusiasm."
- Ralph Waldo Emerson

"You can be greater than anything that can happen to you."
- Norman Vincent Peale

"Realize that you can in and of yourself do much to make yourself a healthy, vital and alive individual."
- Norman Vincent Peale

"...life's a gift, and I don't intend on wasting it. You don't know what hand you're gonna get dealt next. You learn to take life as it comes at you...to make each day count."
- Leonardo DiCaprio

"Whatever you do is what shall be."
- Betty White

"It's not the hand that feeds you, it's the heart that beats for you."
- A Wise Mother

"Nothing worth doing is easy."
- My Loving Husband

"Nobody in life gets exactly what they thought they were going to get, but if you work really hard and you're kind, amazing things will happen ..."
- Conan O'Brien

"It's not only the love of a husband, a wife or children that can enable morale to remain strong and slow the progression of illness, but also the simple love and caring attention of friends old and new."
- David Schreiber

About the Author

First and foremost, Lisa Phillips is a proud
wife and mother. When not chasing after her
three-year-old son, Lisa also enjoys working
as a speech and language pathologist in
Central Massachusetts. She and her husband,
Dennis, happily reside in the Worcester area
with their son, Bryce. She can be contacted at
lisamphillips@gmail.com. This is her first
book publication.

CPSIA information can be obtained
at www.ICGtesting.com
Printed in the USA
BVHW041454240119
538599BV00008B/55/P

9 781453 672877